Diary

of a

Red Sox Season

—— 2007 ——

Johnny Pesky
with
Maureen Mullen

TRIUMPH
B O O K S

For Dad, who as a 10-year-old in the hospital
once told my grandmother he couldn't talk to her
because the Red Sox were on the radio and Ted Williams
was on deck (meaning Johnny Pesky was at bat);
and for Mom, who would have gotten a kick out of this.

M.A.M.

This book is available in quantity at special discounts for your group or organization. For further information, contact:

Triumph Books
542 South Dearborn Street
Suite 750
Chicago, Illinois 60605
(312) 939-3330
Fax (312) 663-3557

Printed in U.S.A.

ISBN: 978-1-60078-068-4

Design by Sue Knopf

All photos by Brita Meng Outzen

Contents

Foreword • v

Acknowledgments • viii

The Off-Season • 1

Spring Training • 9

April • 17

May • 37

June • 53

July • 81

August • 101

September • 125

The Postseason • 173

About the Authors • 216

Foreword

OPENING DAY AT FENWAY PARK IN 2005 was one of the most memorable moments in New England sports history. It was the day the world championship banner was raised in center field, the Red Sox's own star-spangled banner symbolizing the end to 86 years without a world championship, right before the distribution of the World Series rings to players from that 2004 team, as well as generations of Red Sox players that bridged the franchise from 1918 to 2004.

Joe Torre, Derek Jeter, and the Yankees stood on the top step of the visiting dugout in respect for the team that came back from a 3–0 deficit in the American League Championship Series, and, as Jeter said, "As a reminder of what we want." But the most memorable moment came when Johnny Pesky was introduced and walked out of the dugout toward the podium to be handed his ring. He received the biggest ovation of the entire ceremony— more than David Ortiz or Curt Schilling—and as the roar of the crowd rolled across The Fens, Torre and Jeter led the Yankees in what was a raucous, wild show of emotion. "Johnny Pesky is one of the most respected people in our game," said Torre. "Seeing him walk out there and hearing the response of the crowd gave me chills. I almost shed a tear. I didn't like seeing the Red Sox get those rings, but the moment for Johnny Pesky was special—for me, for Derek, for anyone who loves and respects baseball."

On a day many New Englanders never thought would happen, Johnny Pesky received the greatest ovation from Red Sox fans. There have been greater players in the interregnum. He last played for the Red Sox in 1952, before being traded to the Tigers, but he never left Boston. He never stopped adoring the franchise even though his two-year managerial reign was cut short by slovenly players and even worse management, and, most of all, he never stopped being good to people. Pesky and his late wife, Ruthie, could go to a card show, a Bosox Club luncheon, or stop at The Hilltop Steak House on Route 1 in Saugus, and they were always known as the kindest people any Red Sox fan ever met. "No one," former Red Sox owner John Harrington once said, "better represented the Boston Red Sox. In many ways, he *is* the Red Sox."

For years Pesky has had the clubhouse locker right inside the door to the right as one walks in. He sits and chats with players, the media, Terry Francona, and coaches, and he goes out on the field during batting practice. "Having Johnny here is part of understanding what it means to play for the Red Sox," said Mike Lowell.

So 2007 was a wondrous season for Pesky and the Red Sox. It was a team of personalities, like David Ortiz and Manny Ramirez. It had youthful exuberance in Jonathan Papelbon, Dustin Pedroia, Jacoby Ellsbury, and Jon Lester. It had rock-solid men whose lives are based in values, Jason Varitek, Mike Timlin, Mike Lowell, and Alex Cora. They ran out to a big lead in the American League East, then spent the rest of the season watching the Yankees grow larger and larger in the rearview mirror, bending but never breaking. They went down 3–1 in the ALCS in Cleveland and never let up, and they eventually beat the Colorado Rockies in four straight games to win the World Series.

Josh Beckett was unquestionably the MVP of the postseason, but to many fans Dustin Pedroia became this generation's Johnny Pesky. Pedroia is barely 5′5″ and so cares about winning that after his freshman year at Arizona State gave back his scholarship so the program could sign a couple of pitchers. When ASU finally made the College World Series after he'd left for pro baseball, all the coaches and players had "DP" on their caps in honor of the player who they felt symbolized their success.

What Pedroia meant to Arizona State in a five-year window, Johnny Pesky has symbolized to the Red Sox for 60-something years. As he has his place in the franchise's history, so, too, he had his place with the 2007 team that brought New England its second championship in four years, a place that allowed him a full vision of one of the greatest seasons in the history of The Olde Towne Team.

—Peter Gammons

Acknowledgments

THE AUTHORS WOULD LIKE TO THANK the following for their help and support: the Boston Red Sox; Dr. Charles Steinberg; John Blake; Pam Ganley; Henry Mahegan; Marty Ray; Bob Barr; Nick Cafardo; Larry Corea; Joanne DeVeau; Marcia Dick; Dick Flavin; Dawn-Marie Driscoll; Janet, Charlie, Chris, Meagan, and Connor Ehl; Joe Flanagan; Peter Gammons; Anne Heffernan; Ruth Hickey; Norman Marcus; Brita Meng Outzen; Bob, Ryan, Kevin, Amy, Danny, Timmy, and Jack Mullen (both of them); Rich O'Neill; Mark Pankin; David and Alison Pesky; Rob Reichert; Joe Saccardo; the Salem Diner breakfast crew; Baseball-Almanac.com; Baseball-Reference.com; MLB.com; and Retrosheet.org.

The
Off-Season

Johnny Pesky

December 14, 2006

There is no real off-season for the Boston Red Sox. Today's press conference announcing the signing of Japanese pitching sensation Daisuke Matsuzaka is evidence of that. In addition to the $51.1 million posting fee the Red Sox paid for the rights to negotiate with him, Matsuzaka agreed to terms with the Red Sox on a six-year, $52 million contract. It is safe to say that Fenway Park has never hosted a press conference like this one before. Hundreds of local, national, and international media representatives arrive hours before the 5:00 PM press conference to claim seats in the EMC Club inside the ballpark. Boston mayor Thomas M. Menino is also on hand to welcome the Sox's newest international sensation. Scores of satellite trucks clog the narrow streets outside the ancient ballpark. Red Sox principal owner John Henry calls it a "joyous day in New England."

For Johnny Pesky, the Red Sox legend, the day signals the start of a season unlike any other in his time with the Olde Towne Team—a time that spans parts of eight decades. Pesky, who gave up three playing years—1943, 1944, and 1945—early in his career to serve in the navy during World War II, has often been asked his thoughts on Japanese players coming to the United States. On Matsuzaka's big day, he had nothing but good things to say.

I'VE NEVER SEEN ANYTHING LIKE IT. I think I've seen a lot of press conferences in my time, but nothing like this. There were cameras and flashbulbs everywhere. I thought I was on a movie lot. It was great. You couldn't get up that street. You couldn't move. I wanted to stick around, but I had to leave to take a driving test. I was there when he arrived. I wanted to see him, so I waited as long as I could. Finally he showed up and went into the ballpark. But I thought he handled it very well. He seemed very calm, very respectful. I think he's probably used to a lot of attention.

It's a big thing, and rightfully so. They say he's the best pitcher to ever come from Japan. So he had a good thing going for him over there. I thought he handled it very, very well. I like what I saw. He was very genteel. He had humility. He was very polite. He bowed. I wanted to see what he looked like. He's a nice, clean-looking kid. They always say listen to people you trust, and everybody I talked to liked him. So that's good enough for me.

I don't have any problem with Japanese players coming over here. How could I? My parents came over here to have a better

The December 14, 2006, press conference to announce the signing of Japanese pitching sensation Daisuke ("Dice-K") Matsuzaka caused a major stir in Red Sox Nation.

life. That's what they're doing, too. The thing was, where I came from we had a lot of every nationality. You name it, we had it. We had Japanese and Chinese kids in the neighborhood. So I got to know them. I went to school with them, and the Japanese kids I knew, geez, they were great kids. There were two brothers named Tokami and the Okasakis that lived right in my neighborhood. The Okasakis were twin boys. And the war had been on for six months or so and they went back to Japan. They became flyers and fought in the Japanese Imperial Navy. That's what I heard. And there was the Tokami brothers, Bobby and Ralph. Bobby was a basketball player and Ralph was a baseball player. One went to Oregon State and the other went to Oregon. Those were the days when they put the parents in camps. That was sad. Their parents went in. They were well scrutinized. But they never caused any trouble. I went to school with them. They were my friends. They were in my house, ate my mother's bread. I didn't consider them enemies. I was Catholic. Half of them were Catholics, too. Some of them had the little statues of Buddha in their homes. The Okasaki brothers were the twins, and you had to go up about eight or 10 steps to get to their house. And at the top of the steps they had a Buddha. It was pretty neat. But they were my friends. We went a lot of places together and had no problems. But the sad part was when their parents had to go to internment camps. They separated them there. But in my neighborhood, we weren't separated. We had everyone. We had Japanese, Chinese, Slavs, Germans, Jewish. We had the League of Nations there. And we all got along. It was a different time. Late '30s, early '40s. And most of us were in school.

When they bombed Pearl Harbor, it left a bad taste for a lot of people. In fact, I was coming out of church, coming up on Overton Street. It came on the radio that the Japanese had bombed Pearl Harbor. Now where in the hell was Pearl Harbor? I didn't know. I knew it was somewhere in the Pacific. But I was in Oregon. I was just starting to play ball for the Red Sox.

We had a black family in my neighborhood, the Bells. I went to school with Billy Bell. We were confirmed together. He was a great guy. He went to the University of Oregon and was on ROTC. He went into the air force and became an officer. He had medals all over his chest. But he had a tough time of it when he was in the service down South. When we were kids, he used to come by my house. We'd play together. My mother would bake bread. We'd have some of her bread. "Beeely," she'd call him, with her accent. "Beeely, sit down and have some bread." Turns out that bread saved his life. During the war he was flying over Germany and got shot down. He landed in a field and three guys come to get him. I think they were farmers, not soldiers. So, he doesn't know what to do. So, he says to them, "*Daime kruva,*" which means "Give me bread" in Croatian. He learned that from my mother. "*Daime kruva.*" Those German guys must have been thinking, "We have a black Slav on our hands." Well, he survived. He got to the underground. I think he flew a few more missions. But he made it home safe.

And now we have Japanese players, black players, Latin guys. Everyone's playing for the same team. It's better now. Yes, it's better now.

February 10, 2007

Johnny has just wrapped up fantasy camp, and is waiting for the start of spring training. The week of fantasy camp is as much of a chance for former teammates to get together, reminisce, renew acquaintances, and remember the good old days as it is for the "players" to get a taste of baseball life. Along with fellow Red Sox alumni Jerry Moses, Bill Campbell, Gary Bell, Rick Miller, Steve Crawford, Jim Corsi, Bob Stanley, Lee Stange, Gary Allenson, and Rich Gale, Johnny spent the past week putting wannabes from all walks of life through the paces of big-league baseball. Well, sort of.

YEAH, THAT'S A BUNCH OF OLD GUYS TRYING TO PLAY BALL. Someone always gets hurt. You got muscles and stuff popping all over the place. It's a fun time. There're a lot of young guys in there, too. A lot of frustrated ballplayers out there. I have a friend who's a lawyer from San Francisco. He's a great Red Sox fan. He brings his wife and one of his sons and some other friends. They come out every year. They play ball every day, and then we get together to have dinner at night. They have a helluva time. The funniest thing I ever saw was a father pitching to his son. The father was in his 80s, the son was in his 60s. He threw the ball pretty good. That was two years ago.

We have a kangaroo court. Everybody gets fined for something. You looked to right field and you should have looked to left field, you get a fine. Everything goes to the Jimmy Fund. [The Jimmy Fund supports childhood cancer research and care at the Dana-Farber Cancer Institute.] But it's a good time. There are a lot of wealthy guys who show up. Sometimes they pick up the tab for the whole team. If the team gets fined, the rich guy just gives a credit card. There are about eight or 10 teams. For coaches and managers you get all us ex–Red Sox players. You get a lot of pulled muscles. We always tell them to take it easy, especially on the first day. But nobody does. Some guys are in pretty good shape. The best part of the whole thing is at dinner when they give out all the fines. You'd think you're in a big-league camp. It's pretty funny to watch. You can't argue a fine or then it gets doubled. Well, you can try. You say, "I appeal." But if you lose the appeal, it costs you $2 instead of $1. But it's all good-natured. And no one ever squawks. The players know they're going to get fined for something. If you have 15 guys on your team and 10 get fined, somebody says, "Okay, who didn't get fined? Raise your hand." And then you get fined for not getting fined.

You meet the people and they all want to talk baseball. I still hear from some people throughout the year. They're very friendly, nice people. We get some women. Janet Miller, Rick Miller's wife, she's pretty good. We had a little Japanese girl. She played the infield. She wasn't very good, but she tried. There're about two or three Asians, some Latins, mostly Americans. And everyone gets along. By the third day you'd think they were friends all their lives.

I like it because it gets me ready for spring training.

Spring
Training

*Johnny
Pesky*

February 16, 2007

Pitchers and catchers officially report to Fort Myers for spring training today. Daisuke Matsuzaka held his first spring-training press conference last night, at City of Palms Park. Although it didn't quite reach the fever pitch of that December press conference at Fenway Park, with approximately 150 media members in attendance here in Florida there is definitely no shortage of interest in the Japanese star.

I'M ANXIOUS TO SEE THE NEW JAPANESE PITCHER. I didn't go to his press conference last night, but I heard it was quite a scene. I can't wait to see him pitch. He's supposed to be something. He's got that pitch, what's it called, a gyroball? Something like that. I have no idea what that could be. I'm glad I don't have to face him.

9

I'm really excited to see this team. They made some good pickups this year. It will be exciting to see everyone once they get here. I always look forward to spring training. Oh, sure. I used to love it because I was much more active, but now we bring so many coaches…but I do a few things. And then I get to meet all the fans. That's always fun. But I can't wait to get going. The best part about it is everyone comes in, you haven't seen people for a while, and you see them again, and it's like you haven't even missed a beat. And once you get going with the workouts, it's just great to be out there on the field, in the sun. I always look forward to spring training.

February 20, 2007

The Red Sox work out at the minor league complex at the end of Edison Avenue, about two miles from City of Palms Park, where the Sox play their spring-training games. All the players work out here. There are five fields at the minor league complex. One field is named for Eddie Popowski, who spent 65 years in the Red Sox organization before his death in 2001 at the age of 88. Another field is named for Pesky. The big leaguers work out in the morning and the minor leaguers take over in the afternoon.

Spring training is a baseball fan's paradise. In one day, several hundred baseball players will work out at the complex. While tickets to games at City of Palms Park are difficult to get—the Sox have sold out every game at City of Palms since March 16, 2003—admission to workouts is free. Knowledgeable fans scout prime real estate near the white fence outside the clubhouse where players take turns signing autographs after

Getting an autograph from the always-gracious Johnny Pesky is one of the highlights for Red Sox fans attending spring-training workouts.

workouts. Johnny is set up on a folding chair inside the first-base dugout of one field. There is a line of autograph seekers from the time he sits down until after the workouts conclude three or four hours later. Johnny will be there for hours every day, until just about everyone has gotten an autograph from or had a picture taken with the legend. The last thing he'd want to do is disappoint anyone.

I REALLY ENJOY IT. I DO. IT'S FUN TO MEET PEOPLE. I'll tell the little kids, "You don't remember me playing, but your parents do." And then I have to remember that their parents probably don't. It's their grandparents. But I really enjoy it. They're great. They're all very nice and very complimentary to me. Some of the folks will say, "Johnny, I remember when you did this or that." And I say, "You do? You must be as old as me!" It's a lot of fun. I don't work as much as I used to. So I sit over here and sign autographs and talk to people. But I really enjoy it. I guess people like it, too. I guess they wouldn't stop by if they didn't want to. I think signing autographs is part of the job. I always did. That's part of the deal. I've always thought that. My rookie year, my brother came to Boston to see me and we're leaving the park after the game. And we're going up Lansdowne Street and there were some kids out by the gate. We're going to Kenmore Square to get something to eat. My brother grabbed me by the arm and says, "Sign these things." They all had pennants and things. So instead of getting down there in 10 minutes it took us a half hour. But that was okay. I didn't mind at all.

Ha! I remember the first time someone asked me for an autograph. I thought they were kidding! I said, "Are you sure?" But the fans here have been very, very good to me. Excellent. I couldn't ask for anything better. People come up and ask for autographs or pictures, and it's fun. It really is. People say, "My grandfather saw you play, Johnny." I say, "Really?" And they flatter the hell out of me. "You were this and you were that." It's very flattering.

February 28, 2007

The Red Sox's first spring-training game is tonight at City of Palms Park against the Minnesota Twins, whose spring-training home is on the other side of Fort Myers at the Lee County Sports Complex. There are a lot of jokes about the Mayor's Cup, awarded to the team that wins the spring series between the two teams. The Red Sox are looking to avenge the Twins' Mayor's Cup victory last year. As he did at the minor league complex, Johnny will resume his autograph-signing duties before every home game, sitting for hours in a folding chair near the stands on the third-base side.

THIS IS ALWAYS FUN. I ALWAYS LOOK FORWARD to spring training. You see people you haven't seen in a long time. There are people who come down to spring training every year for vacation. It's nice to see them coming back every year. They stop by and say hello. The whole atmosphere of spring training is just different. And it sure beats being back home, where it's cold! We'll play teams we don't see during the season, and we'll see young guys just starting out who might get in for a game or two. I look forward to when the Dodgers come here. I'll see Tommy Lasorda, I think, if he makes the trip. But yes, spring training is one of my favorite times.

I always look forward to this time of year, when the games start. I can see some of the older guys, the veterans who've been around for a while, and some of the kids and the new guys. It's fun to watch the new guys because sometimes I've heard of them, but maybe I haven't seen them before. We got a new shortstop this year, [Julio] Lugo. I'm anxious to see him out there. We've got a bunch of new pitchers. The two kids from Japan. Matsuzaka, he's the righty, the starter. He's been marvelous to watch so far. He handles everything so well. We've got

Spring training is a time to renew old friendships. Here, Johnny Pesky visits with the man he calls the all-time best Red Sox shortstop, Nomar Garciaparra (left), and former Sox (and current Dodger) manager, Grady Little.

another Japanese kid, the lefty [Hideki] Okajima. I don't know much about him. So it will be fun to see him in games. We've got a bunch of new relievers

[Brendan] Donnelly, [J.C.] Romero, [Joel] Pineiro. We've got the workhorse back, [Curt] Schilling. [Josh] Beckett's back. [Jason] Varitek, Papi [David Ortiz], Manny [Ramirez], [Mike] Lowell. When you look around, we've got a pretty good team. Drew in right field. He's new. He's a great athlete. When you look at every position, this is a very good baseball team. Papelbon. He's solid. He was in the bullpen last year. But he'll be fine no matter where he pitches.

I like watching the kids, too. We've got some exciting kids. The little second baseman, [Dustin] Pedroia. [Jacoby] Ellsbury, he looks real good. He's another Oregon boy, so that says something right there! And I'm really happy to see Jon Lester. [Lester was diagnosed with lymphoma in 2006, but his cancer is now in remission.] I'm just happy he's here and healthy. That's a helluva thing to go through, and he looks great. Yes, I think we've got a very good team.

March 26, 2007

The Sox enter the last week of spring training with games against the Reds, the Pirates, the Twins, and the Devil Rays before heading to Philadelphia for two games with the Phillies.

Most baseball people caution against reading too much into spring-training performances. If a team does well in the spring, that doesn't necessarily translate into a strong regular-season performance. And if a player is slow to get going, that doesn't automatically mean he'll have a hard time once the season starts.

THE LAST TWO SPRINGS ARE THE TWO BEST SPRING TRAININGS I've ever been to—the way [bench coach] Brad Mills and [manager] Terry [Francona] got together and ran things. Everything was organized, especially the eight to 10 days before the games just to get in shape. I thought the program was the best I ever saw. Years ago, you used to come in there like a bunch of sheep, and you'd try to get them all together. But right now, I think baseball is so well educated and organized—better than it's been at any

The Japanese press turned out in full force for Red Sox spring training in Fort Myers, Florida, to see new American Leaguer Daisuke Matsuzaka.

time in our history. That's the way I feel. And I think right now Terry's got great people around him. We got some new guys in. The pitching coach [John Farrell] seems very good, very smart. The hitting coach [Dave Magadan].

You know who I thought was a good manager? Ralph Houk. He didn't get credit for it, but he had success with the Yankees. See, when you change clubs, you gain a reputation. They expect you to be like you were, and that's not always the case. You have different personnel. I loved him when he was with the Red Sox. I worked for him when he was in the minor leagues.

But I'm really looking forward to the season. I feel very good about this team. I always feel good about this team.

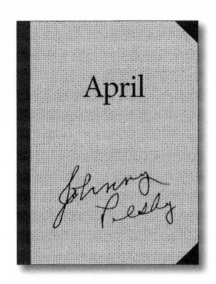

April

April 2, 2007

This year marks the 67th anniversary of Johnny's signing with the Boston Red Sox, a career that spans eight decades. It is unlikely that any player will ever be affiliated with one team for that long ever again.

The Red Sox open the season in Kansas City against the Royals. Things start out rough for the Sox, as they fall to the Royals 7–1. Curt Schilling has a difficult outing, going four innings, allowing five runs on eight hits and two walks, and striking out five. Reliever Hideki Okajima is inhospitably welcomed to the big leagues by John Buck, sending the Japanese import's first pitch over the center-field wall for a home run.

WELL, THAT WAS TOUGH TO SEE. We don't like to start the season out like that. That was a tough one for Schilling. That's a tough one for Okajima, too. You don't like to see a guy start out like that. But it goes to show you, he's a pretty good pitcher, but on any day anyone can get you. But I like him. He's got that really funny delivery. He'll be okay.

And you have to remember, it's just one game. A lot of people think Opening Day will tell you how the season will go. But that's just nonsense. It's one game. It's a loss. But we'll be right back out there tomorrow.

April 4, 2007

The Red Sox home opener is less than a week away. But, unlike previous years, Johnny will not be in the dugout during home games. Major League Baseball is enforcing the rule limiting the number of coaches allowed in the dugout during games to six. The rule applies from Opening Day until August 31, when rosters expand and teams can add a coach. Johnny has heard from his legion of fans, who are disappointed that they won't see the legend in the dugout this year. A few have written to the commissioner asking him to review the decision. Some have started petitions in the hope of getting the decision overturned. While Johnny is disappointed, he understands the decision is not directed at him and is being enforced throughout baseball. He will, of course, abide by the decision, he says, and would never want to do anything to embarrass the team or the game that has meant so much to him throughout his life.

WELL, I'M VERY DISAPPOINTED. But I understand. I'll do whatever they want me to. Whatever they tell me. I'll still be around, and I'll be in uniform before the game. I'll sign autographs. I'll clean the dugout. I don't care. But I would never say anything bad. It's a decision. It's not just me. It's all teams. Maybe they'll change their minds. But the Red Sox have always been good to me. This game has been good to me. It's my life and I would never want to say or do anything to embarrass myself, or the team, or the game. People ask me about it, and I just say, "What can I do?" I'm happy for all the support people have shown me. But it's a rule, and I've always abided by baseball rules. It's nice that people say they will miss me. I appreciate that. But I ain't going anywhere. I'll still be around.

The Red Sox beat the Royals in Kansas City, 7–1, evening their record at 1–1, a half game behind the Yankees.

April 10, 2007

It's opening Day at Fenway Park. After their season-opening trip through Kansas City and Texas, the Red Sox bring a 3–3 record into the home opener. It is cool and cloudy with a strong wind blowing in from right field.

The Red Sox are hosting a season-long celebration of the 1967 Impossible Dream team, with members of that star-crossed squad taking the field for pregame ceremonies. Twenty-three members of the '67 team wearing full uniforms emerge from behind a giant American flag hanging from the Green Monster. Billy Conigliaro, who played for the Sox from 1969–71, represents his brother Tony, whose promising career was derailed when he was hit in the face with a pitch in August 1967; he died in 1990. Robert Goulet, a native of Lawrence, Massachusetts, sings "The Impossible Dream."

The Red Sox celebrate Fenway Park's Opening Day 2007 by having several members of the 1967 "Impossible Dream" team throw out the ceremonial first pitch.

While the regular-season opener is special, it doesn't really "count" if it takes place on the road. The season truly begins when Fenway Park hosts its own Opening Day.

The Sox beat the Mariners, 14–3, improving their season record to 4–3—they are tied with the Yankees and the Blue Jays for first place in the American League East.

OH, YEAH. YES, YOU LIVE FOR THIS DAY. You get through spring training. You're all refreshed. The enthusiasm of the crowd—it's just great. You look up in the crowd, you see people that you knew through the years. They're back here every year. It's wonderful to see them. Opening Day is special. It really is. I don't even know how many I've had, but every one is special. And I always look forward to the next one. Opening on the road just doesn't really count. Well, of course, the games count. But it just doesn't feel like Opening Day until it's at Fenway. Nope, I'll wait till I get home. That's the real one. Opening at Fenway, that's the one that counts. That's the real one. It's a wonderful feeling. I think the Boston Opening Day, you could live your whole life and never have that feeling anywhere else. That's my feeling ever since I've been here.

And you get such good crowds during the season. They get so excited. The fans here are great. They're yelling and screaming from before the game starts until the final out. You don't get that everywhere. I've seen Opening Days a few other places, and they're just not the same. And if we win on Opening Day, it's even that much better.

Seeing that team come back today, that was something. I wasn't with the Sox in 1967. I was with Pittsburgh. So I wasn't here for all of that, but of course I followed it. I was still living here. So I saw it and I followed it. It was something. It was nice to see them all today. Dick Williams, Yaz [Carl Yastrzemski], Rico [Petrocelli], Jim Lonborg, Mike Andrews, Reggie Smith, Gary Bell, Lee Stange. That was quite a team. I really liked Lonborg. When I saw him pitch, I said, "Boy, I wish I could have played in his era." I thought he was the closest thing to Tex Hughson. He threw with his heart. He was a big, strong guy. He was great. They had a great team that year. But unfortunately, they had the same bad luck we had against the Cardinals in '46.

But we won today, and that's what's important. I'll take it.

April 15, 2007

And Julio Lugo makes five—five years, five different Red Sox shortstops. Nomar Garciaparra, Pokey Reese, Edgar Renteria, Alex Gonzalez, and now Lugo, who agreed to a four-year, $36 million contract with the Sox during the off-season.

A GOOD SHORTSTOP HAS TO HAVE GOOD HANDS. You always hear that. But if you have good hands, that means you understand how a ball might react when it's hit as it approaches you. Some guys have that knack. Bobby Doerr had that knack. He wasn't a shortstop. He was a second baseman, but he had great hands. He knew how to read a ball. Brooks Robinson had that knack. He was a third baseman. Phil Rizzuto had that knack. Pee Wee Reese had it. I wish I could say Pesky had that knack, but I wasn't in their class. I was an adequate shortstop. I wasn't one that you'd rave about. I had a decent arm. I didn't have a rifle, but I could get the ball over there. I got rid of the ball quickly. I knew how to play, when to shorten up, when to play deep, things like that. And you learn from the manager and your teammates, they've seen all these guys. You've just got to pay attention. Of all the shortstops back then, Vern Stephens, geez, he was tough. He was more suited for third base. We flip-flopped a couple of times. He had a great arm.

The position has really changed over the years. When I played, you'd see a lot of little guys like me and Rizzuto. It's a lot of big guys now. We didn't have a lot of big guys playing shortstop back then.

Of all the Red Sox shortstops I've seen, it's tough to say who would be the best. We've had a few, but I'd say Nomar. He did everything. He could hit. He could run. He could throw.

I like this guy we got now, Lugo. I think he's going to be very good out there. He could be a very good-hitting shortstop, but he has a tendency to swing at pitches that aren't strikes, I think. But he's still young, and once he learns that, he's going to be very good. He's got a wonderful body. He's very fast. He's got a fine arm.

Today's game against the Angels at Fenway Park was postponed because of rain. The Sox are 6–4, tied with the Blue Jays (at 7–5) for the American League East lead.

April 20, 2007

The Red Sox are hosting the New York Yankees for a three-game weekend series, the two teams' first meeting of the season. Yankees third baseman Alex Rodriguez has set a blistering early pace, batting .351, slugging .965, and hitting 10 home runs and 26 RBIs.

It's early in the season, but that is never an issue when these two teams meet. There's always a special buzz in the air when the Yankees come to town.

The Sox take the first game of the series, 7–6, scoring five runs in the eighth, and Coco Crisp picks up a two-RBI triple. Okajima picks up his first save of the season. The Sox are 1½ games up on the Orioles and two games ahead of the Yankees in the American League East.

THERE'S ALWAYS SOMETHING SPECIAL about these games with the Yankees. I go back to when we played. We had some good teams, both of us. We always wanted to beat the hell out of them. We didn't like them. We didn't like losing to them. But there was a respect. We knew they had some very good players over there. But you know what? We had some pretty good players over here. You look over the years at these two teams. There have been some really good games. We had some tough times and some bad breaks sometimes. But somehow, it seemed like we always had good games against them. But oh, yeah, I always love beating the Yankees! They're always such a good team. You know if you beat them, you got a pretty good team, too.

April 21, 2007

In the second inning of tonight's 7–5 win over the Yankees, Coco Crisp and Alex Cora eventually come around to score after knocking back-to-back bunt hits off New York's Jeff Karstens; it's believed to be only the seventh time since 1967 that a pair of Sox have managed consecutive bunt hits, and the first time since 1994. Of the other six times, a Sox duo went back-to-back bunting four times in the seventh inning, once in the fifth, and once to lead off a game. Twice the feat was accomplished at Fenway Park, four times on the road. The other Sox pairs to hit consecutive bunts were Doug Griffin and Lynn McGlothen in the fifth off the Yankees' Rob Gardner on September 13, 1972, in New York; Tommy Harper and Luis Aparicio in the seventh off the Yankees' Fritz Peterson on April 14, 1973, in New York; Cecil Cooper and Denny Doyle in the seventh off Milwaukee's Rick Austin on September 14, 1975, at Fenway; Rick Burleson and

Coco Crisp lays down the first of two back-to-back bunt singles in the seventh inning of the April 21, 2007, tilt at Fenway, helping lead the Sox to a 7–5 win over the Yankees.

Denny Doyle in the seventh off Baltimore's Fred Holdsworth on October 1, 1976, at Fenway; Mike Greenwell and Rick Miller in the seventh off the Orioles' Brad Havens on October 3, 1985, in Baltimore; and Otis Nixon, leading off the game, and Tim Naehring off the A's Ron Darling on July 16, 1994, in Oakland.

The Sox beat the Yankees, 7–5, holding their 1½-game lead over the Orioles and dropping the Yankees to three games back in the division.

BUNTING AND SPEED CAN REALLY CHANGE A GAME. Being able to handle the bat is so important, as is being able to get on base. We won tonight by two runs, and those two guys both scored after bunting. You don't see guys bunting for hits very often now. But at the right point in the game, it can really make a difference. You get the element of surprise on your side. I'm sure their pitcher wasn't expecting the first bunt, and he probably wasn't expecting the second one either. But these two guys are very good bunters, and they've got speed too. They're probably the fastest guys we've had around here for a while. In fact, they're definitely the fastest two guys we've had here in a long time. It was as if, after Coco bunted, Cora said, "Oh yeah? I can do that too."

And it's fun to watch. The crowd gets into it, probably because they don't see it very often. When I played, we had Dominic [DiMaggio] leading off, and then me, and then Ted Williams came up after us. We knew if we had both of us on, there was a good chance at least one of us was going to score—and a lot of times both of us scored. Our job was to get on base. A lot of times we got a hit, sometimes we walked, sometimes we'd try the bunt. But you got that element of surprise on your side and the next thing you know, you got a couple of guys on base and in scoring position.

Dominic and I had a hit-and-run play and we had a bunt-and-run play. There was a point when our hit-and-run just seemed like it wasn't working for us. So I said to Dominic, "Let's try that bunt-and-run play that we've talked about." When I went to my nose, that was the sign for the hit-and-run, and when I went to the top of my cap, that meant bunt-and-run. But what Dom could do, if he knew we were going to bunt-and-run, he'd get out as far as he could, take as big a lead as he could, and as soon as the ball went to the plate, he was jumping. He could see the ball go to the plate, and I could really bunt. I'm proud of that. I could really kill the ball. That would bring the third baseman in, and Dom would take a look. He'd see the third baseman's coming in to field the bunt and throw me out, and I'm getting Dominic to second with Williams and [Vern] Stephens and [Bobby] Doerr coming up. Now, we'd usually try this with nobody out, sometimes with one out. So, now he's going to second, and sees there's no one covering third, and he just keeps on going.

We worked this about four days in a row. So now the Yankees are in town, and we try it on them. Bill Dickey is catching. I think Bobby Brown was playing third base. But in the meantime, this bunt-and-run play we had got in the papers. So there we are. We're in a tough game. We try the bunt-and-run. I laid down a perfect bunt. Brown fields it, and he throws me out at first. Well, Dominic is making like a jackrabbit for third. He could run. As Brown throws me out, before Dom could slow up and stop at second, he's heading for third. But guess what, so is Dickey. He's waiting there to tag Dom out. He says to Dom, "I gotcha!" Then he says, "Yeah, guess what, I read the papers too." Well, that was pretty funny. I guess I didn't think so at the time. But it seems pretty funny now.

I was a ground-ball hitter. Unless you get a ball that you can jerk—and I had that kind of a swing—the idea of a hit-and-run is to get the runner to second base. We worked it a lot. Dominic scored over 100 runs most years, I scored over 100 runs [for each of his first six seasons]. I think we did that five or six years, and Williams drove us in.

We talked a lot in the clubhouse. We'd just sit and talk, and listen to Ted tell us how to hit. He was our hitting instructor. He could just see things and correct them. It was so easy for him. And he loved us. But it was so much fun playing in those years. Geez, we had a lot of fun. It was wonderful.

Our job was just to get Ted to the plate. If the count was 3–0, I was always taking. If I got to 3–1, then I had two pitches to work with. If it was 2–2, I'd look for a bad ball to make it 3–2, and if it's 3–2, well, I figured I was still in the driver's seat. Just get the ball on the ground. Get the guy into scoring position. Just slap at it. I learned that hanging around the clubhouse when I worked for the Portland team in the [Pacific] Coast League when I was in high school. Today, well, I can talk a good game, but that's about it!

April 22, 2007

The Red Sox complete a three-game sweep of the Yankees at Fenway Park for the first time since 1990. The 7–6 victory features four consecutive home runs in the bottom of the third, tying a major league record. Manny Ramirez starts the show of power with a mammoth drive over everything in left-center field onto Lansdowne Street. J.D. Drew follows with a blast into the bleachers beyond the Sox bullpen in right-center. Mike Lowell is next with a blast over the Monster, tying the game, and Jason Varitek puts the exclamation point on with a laser into the Monster seats.

There's always something special about beating the Yankees. And sometimes there's something for the history books too.

Riding a five-game winning streak, the Sox are 12–5 on the season, 1½ games ahead of the Orioles, four games up on the Yankees.

I'VE NEVER SEEN ANYTHING LIKE THAT. I've seen Ted [Williams], [Vern] Stephens, and [Bobby] Doerr do it, but not four in a row. Three in a row is very rare. But four in a row? Wow! I never had to worry too much about hitting home runs. I was happy with the couple I got [17 in his major league career]. I was lucky if I got four in a year [the most Johnny hit was three in a year]. I think it would be rather disturbing for a young pitcher to give up home runs like that, but that's the game and you have to deal with it. After two are hit, you step off the mound and say, "Well, this isn't going to happen again." And then after the third one, you say, "There's no way it can happen again. I could throw one right down the middle, it couldn't happen again." But when you got good hitters like we have, they're dangerous. But, as a pitcher, you just put it behind you and bounce back. You have to.

I think the hitters are much better today than we had. They're much bigger. We were a bunch of little guys. But you always look for a guy who can play. You don't have to be a big guy. You just have to have the ability. Rizzuto was a little guy. There're a lot of little guys who can play the game.

But watching four home runs like that, when it's your team, that's ecstasy. It's just a lot of fun, and it really brings a lot of

Jason Varitek helps secure a power-fueled sweep of the Yankees with the last of four consecutive home runs (tying an MLB record) in the third inning on April 22, 2007.

excitement to your team. And you know, it's always special to beat the Yankees. They always had the big cheeses. So it's always fun to beat them. It helps your pride and your vanity, but it's fun. It was like an imaginary war with them when we played. We never tried to kill anybody, but we always wanted to beat them. We played hard.

I'll give you an example. When we got back after the service, guys would run in, trying to break up a double play. [Joe] DiMaggio got me in Boston one time and he hurt me. It wasn't bad, but he took me out. Rang my bell a little bit. And he hurt my vanity. About 10 days later, we're in Yankee Stadium. And he was a good guy. When he was in the field, he'd take his gum out and throw it at me. He's on first base with one out. It's about the third or fourth inning and Tommy Henrich is hitting behind him. He was a left-handed hitter and he always pulled the ball. So, I hollered over to Bobby [Doerr], "If the ball's hit to you, give it to me quick." Sure enough, third pitch, Bobby gets it. It was hit so good, I'm waiting for DiMaggio. I wanted to tag him right there [in the forehead], but I hit him right there [in the shoulder]. So he said, "Well, I guess we're even now, huh?" I said, "We are like hell! You damn near killed me in Boston last week, you little dago!" But he just laughed it off. He just brushed off my tag like it was a mosquito. I get a kick out of telling that story because it's true. And he used to call me "you little shit." But I figured he wouldn't think of that after I tagged him. But he wasn't a dirty player. He'd come in. He was so strong.

There was a guy with the White Sox. I hated him. He'd kick at you. He had those spikes and he'd want to cut you. Taffy Wright. He was a mean guy. We'd take a guy out but we'd use our bodies. We had some head hunters, but when they wanted to hit you, they'd hit you in the rear end. They wouldn't throw around your head mostly. But sometimes, you get a guy who's mean, they'll do that. I remember one time in Detroit, Dizzy Trout is pitching for the Tigers. He's a big guy. He threw awful hard. He threw one in close. I was hitting in front of Ted. I took two steps toward the mound. He took two steps toward me and said,

"Don't worry. It'll get up there soon enough." And the next pitch is under my chin and he looks at me and says, "Was that close enough?" But he was a great guy. He was a wonderful guy.

It was always when we played the Yankees, Detroit, the White Sox. Detroit had excellent pitching. They had [Virgil] Trucks, Trout, [Hal] Newhouser, Frank Lary. Goddamn, they had good pitching! We went to New York, you looked at Whitey Ford, Turley, four or five more guys. But I think the pitching now is every bit as good as when we played. I think they throw harder. But the guys playing today are bigger, stronger. Even the little guys are strong.

April 23, 2007

Pulitzer Prize–winning writer David Halberstam, the author of a heart-warming tribute to Johnny, Ted Williams, Bobby Doerr, and Dom DiMaggio, died today in a car accident in California.

IT'S A SHAME. IT REALLY IS. He was a nice man and a great writer. It really bothers us. He wrote the book about the four of us. It was very flattering. I know it was a bestseller for a number of years. I was very sad to hear what happened. Just a fine man, a great author, a great writer. He did everything a good human being could possibly do. He was just an outstanding man, and I feel really badly about this. I haven't talked to Dominic or Bobby yet. I hope to tonight when I go home. He spoke exceptionally well. He had that great voice.

He wrote the book, and how that came about was Halberstam was in Florida when Dominic was there. Halberstam found out Dominic was in the area, so he called him and Dominic invited him over to the house and that's how this book came about. He talked to Dominic and Dominic told him we were going to go to Florida to see Ted. He said, "Boy, this will be a great book." He spent quite a bit of time with us. He was very thorough. He called on the phone, showed up at the house. And he did it with Dom, Bobby, and me. I think he fell in love with Dominic. And Dominic, of course, was the smartest of all of us. He looked to Dominic for all his help. I really feel bad about this. Here's a guy who wrote a great book about four old guys.

The Sox lose to the Blue Jays, 7–3, at Fenway. They are now 12–6 for the season. The Orioles are still 1½ games back, while the Jays have climbed into third place, 3½ games out, and the Yankees are four games behind.

April 30, 2007

It's a fine line for a manager, a balancing act really—knowing when to let a player who is scuffling play through those struggles, showing your confidence in him, while hoping he finds a rhythm and works his way out of the slump himself. Or you can sit him, hoping to break the grip of whatever physical or mental gremlins have taken their hold. Francona recently faced that decision with center fielder Crisp, who is mired in a 4-for-36 batting slump for a .111 average through the season's first 10 games. Francona sits Crisp for five games, returning him to the lineup for the three games in New York, in which Crisp goes 4-for-12 with one RBI, three runs scored, a stolen base, and a triple. The Sox take two of three in the Bronx, giving them a 5–1 edge in the season series. Maybe the rest jump-started Crisp. Maybe he was going to break out soon anyway. There's no simple solution and no one fix for a struggling player.

WELL, IT'S NOT A BAD IDEA, BUT YOU GOT TO GET HIM BACK IN the lineup and you got to get him some extra hitting. Or get some guy, one of your coaches, who you have confidence in, who can show this hitter certain things. You don't have to be a Rhodes Scholar. I always watch how they hit. All good hitters, like Joe DiMaggio, are right here. Dominic—right there. Square on the ball.

But you have to be careful. You have to deal with different guys differently. You call him into your office. Have a talk. Make him sit for a day, a few days, and observe. Get one of your coaches that you got confidence in. Let him talk to him. Have him study every pitch that's thrown. I'd say, "This is what we'd like you to do. You try that a couple of times." Then if that doesn't work, you could say, "You tell me what you think you should do." And if they get to that, then they understand it. Because when you go to the plate, then it's just the pitcher and you as a hitter. You're not thinking of all these other things.

I learned a lot from Ted Williams. He was probably the best instructor I ever saw. He understood. He'd bark at you. You'd think, geez, he was mad at you. But he was very intent. And there were a lot of guys who looked to him. Dominic hit .300. I hit .300. And he's hitting number three behind us. Dominic would score over 100 runs. I'd score over 100 runs, and Ted's driving in all of our runs.

But it is a bit of a balancing act trying to figure out when to sit a guy or when to let him keep working at it. It's entirely a choice. If you're a baseball guy, you can see that coming. You call him in, say, "Look, I'm just going to give you today and tomorrow off. If you need another day, we'll go from there. But I want you to play." You have to say, "We need you. We need you because you're one of our best players. You're important to this team." I did that with [Jim] Rice all the time. I had him so buffaloed, he didn't dare ask. But he was very good with me. He responded to me. He came to the ballpark early to work with me. He'd say, "Come on, Woody, let's go."

But it's not really a hard decision for a manager to sit a guy. No, not really. All players are going to go through something like that at some time or another. If you know the game and you understand the game, you get to understand the player. Some guys are sensitive to that. They think you're penalizing them. You say, "This is not a penalty. I'm going to play you. I want you to just observe and see what happens and we'll talk about it." Get the coach that you prefer. I used to sit a lot with Jimmy and talk to him about this. And [Don] Zimmer is the guy that pointed it out to me. It started in spring training. He called in and says, "Johnny, I want you to stay with Rice every day. When he gets out on the field, watch him. Let him warm up, watch him. If he goes to the bathroom, you go with him." And Jimmy responded to me. I had [Dwight] Evans in that group, too, when they were just kids. We had those young guys. We had a good ballclub, and you could see within a year that these guys were going to be outstanding players. Evans, [Fred] Lynn, and [Jim] Rice was as good an outfield as we've ever had.

But when you give a guy a break like that, if he's struggling, that's what it is: a break. Let him take a break. Take a deep breath, clear his head. But the player has to have it here [taps his head], and you got to use your noggin. And you got to know the strike zone. Williams always said that. Of course, no one knew the strike zone like he did. And, of course, he was the greatest hitter and he knew how every hitter should be. He says to me, "Johnny, you know, you hit a lot of ground balls." I said, "Well, I do the best I can." But I always hit strikes, and I got a lot of walks, too. Pitchers tried to fool with you. And I tried to hit-and-run a lot, and I could control the bat. Dominic and I, we had great success with the hit-and-run and the bunt-and-run.

And sometimes you might want to use him, the guy that you've been sitting, later in the game as a pinch-hitter. That way, when he goes into the game, he's not thinking about it. He's just in. He goes in, doesn't think about it, doesn't worry about it. And who knows, maybe he gets a hit, and maybe that's what he needs to break the slump.

The Sox are 16–8 with a 3½-game lead over the Blue Jays; the Orioles are five games back, the Devil Rays are 5½ games out, and the Yankees are holding a very unfamiliar spot in the division basement, 6½ games back.

May

May 3, 2007

The Red Sox win, beating the Mariners 8–7 in a makeup of the April 12 rainout. Starter Daisuke Matsuzaka struggles with his control again in his third consecutive start, allowing seven earned runs on five hits and five walks and striking out one in five innings of work. Matsuzaka is not involved in the decision, his first no-decision in his six starts this season. Manny Ramirez, although hitting just .235, is largely responsible for the win, going 2-for-5 with two runs scored and three RBIs. Manny's two hits are both home runs, including the eventual game winner, a solo shot in the eighth inning. The Sox are now 18–9, for a .667 winning percentage, 5½ games ahead of the Devil Rays, the Blue Jays, and the Yankees, and 6½ games in front of the Orioles.

The Red Sox set a new (post–World War II) single-game attendance record with a crowd of 37,216. The Sox have sold

out every game since May 15, 2003, the second-longest sell-
out streak in Major League Baseball history (behind Cleveland's
stretch of 455 consecutive sellouts from June 12, 1995, through
April 2, 2001). They are on pace to set a new club attendance
record for the eighth consecutive season, a Major League
Baseball record in itself.

THE CROWDS AT FENWAY PARK were always very good when
we played. They were always very baseball-minded. We drew
pretty well in the years when I played, especially after the war
[World War II], because we had good teams and we were always
in contention. We didn't win 100 games every year, but we came
close a couple of times. My first year, in '42, we won 93 games, I
think it was [93–59, with a .612 winning percentage]. Then my
second year, in '46—I was gone for three years because of the
war—but my second year, we won 104 games. [The 1946 team
went 104–50, with a .675 winning percentage, second all-time
in Red Sox history in wins and winning percentage behind the
1912 team, which posted a mark of 105–47 with a .691 winning
percentage. Only three Red Sox teams have broken the century
mark in wins; the third was the 1915 team that went 101–50 for
a .669 percentage.] And then after that we came close a couple
of times. We had some very good teams in those years, and we
should have won more than we did, but it didn't happen.

But this is the best I've ever seen as far as attendance. There's
nothing like it, not in Fenway Park history, and even with other
teams. In the years we played, we thought Boston crowds were

Even at the age of 40, Curt Schilling remains one of the most overpowering pitchers in baseball and among the leaders in strikeouts.

better than any other town—New York, Chicago. The only other town that was close was Detroit. They always had good crowds there. But it's very special as a player when you go out and you know the joint is going to be sold out every night. It's a good feeling, because you know you have all those people on your side. But you also know when you got all those eyes watching you, you better perform, you got to bear down a little bit more. That can be tough on some players. [Ted] Williams was great like that. He loved a big crowd. He'd be talking to everyone and yelling at everyone. You'd have loved him. He was so good about things like that, and he was so good with us. He loved Bobby [Doerr] and Dom [DiMaggio] and me. And we got along so well.

But I love coming out here with these crowds. They're into every pitch. They watch every minute. You know they're on your side. It's tough coming in as a visiting player with crowds like that. That's why you got to like that they're on your side.

May 7, 2007

The Sox have an off day. They beat the Twins, 4–3, in Minnesota yesterday, as Curt Schilling improved his record to 4–1 with a 3.28 ERA, going 6.2 innings, allowing three runs on eight hits and two walks, and striking out seven.

Johnny was virtually impossible to strike out during his career, fanning just 218 times in 4,745 at-bats, an average of only one strikeout for almost 22 at-bats. His career high for whiffs was 36, a number he earned as a rookie in 1942 in 620 at-bats, or once every 17 at-bats. His best seasons for avoiding the K were 1951, when he struck out 15 times in 480 at-bats, an average of once every 32 at-bats; and 1949, when he struck out 19 times in 604 at-bats, a 31.78 strikeout-per-at-bat ratio.

THAT WAS VERY IMPORTANT TO ME. I took pride in that. My job was to get on base. Yeah, I'd go two, three weeks and I wouldn't strike out. That's because I choked up. I had a bat I could handle. I knew the strike zone. I didn't try to do anything foolish. I knew what I could do and what I couldn't. I'd just try to hit behind the ball, and if I hit it good, it would find a hole. If I got under it, I popped it up. I hardly ever struck out, though. I put the ball in play. If I hit the ball to the right of shortstop, it was a base hit, because I could run. Dominic [DiMaggio] and I, we both could run, and that's why we had success. And we had the best hitter [Ted Williams] hitting behind us. When he got up, if we were both on, you know damn well one of us was going to score. And if he hit balls to right-center, shit, we'd cross home plate standing up.

I learned bat control by playing pepper. Nobody does that anymore. A lot of people have never even heard of it now. When [former Sox pitchers] Bill Campbell and Tom Burgmeier were here, we used to do that a lot. They'd try to pitch to me and fool around. And I'd say, "Nah, you ain't going to strike me out." They were pretty good about it. But you never see anyone playing pepper anymore. You used to see the signs at all the parks, "No Pepper Allowed." But now you don't see the signs because you don't even see pepper. It's a good tool. You just take a couple of guys. They stand sort of close to you and throw you the ball and you try to hit it back to them. They take turns throwing to you but they're going fast, so you don't get much time in between. It was fun. It was learning how to adjust your bat, and how to handle your bat. They don't do that too much anymore. Young guys like Wade Boggs, Al Kaline, Bobby Richardson. They were all good to work with.

Richardson played for Ralph Houk in Denver. I got to know him out there because that was my first coaching job [in 1955]. I was actually a player/coach. Denver was the Yankees' Triple A team. We had some great young players out there. Richardson, he was the MVP in the World Series when he finally went up there [in 1960 with the Yankees]. Don Larsen was on that club. Darrell Johnson was the catcher. Johnson was a fine player. It was just me and Ralph out there—and then I was with him when he managed the Red Sox. So we had to do everything out there. I threw batting practice, hit infield, hit fungoes. I tried to work with the young guys. It all depends on what kind of a makeup a person has. A lot of guys thought I was full of coke. So, if you thought that, I'd just stay away. But other times I'd try to work with you. I thought I might be able to help. But pepper is a lost art. You don't see it anymore, maybe once in a while, but that's it. I'd like to see kids try it. It's a lot of fun. You should try it.

The Sox are 20–10, with a six-game lead over the Yankees. The Devil Rays are 6½ back, with the Orioles seven games out and the Blue Jays 7½ games behind.

May 13, 2007

The Red Sox stage an improbable ninth-inning comeback against the Orioles at Fenway. After being held to just three hits through eight innings by Baltimore starter Jeremy Guthrie, the Sox enter the bottom of the ninth down 5–0, rallying for six runs and the win, 6–5.

The Sox are 25–11, extending their division lead to eight games over the Orioles and the Yankees, with the Blue Jays and the Devil Rays both 10½ games behind.

IT'S AN AMAZING COMEBACK. But there are so many things that happen in this game. I feel bad for that other pitcher. He had a great game going. But that's baseball. Sometimes you just don't know why things happen. Well, that's the game. But that was fun. You just can't ever count this team out. They're always in it. But that's the way this game is. Sometimes a guy goes out there for five innings and he's given up no hits, then the next inning he gives up four runs and you're saying, "Well, what happened?" Who knows! There's always something. But it happens. And one thing about baseball is you jut can't take it for granted because so many things can happen and that's the beauty of baseball.

May 15, 2007

Matsuzaka (5–2) wins his fourth straight decision, defeating the Tigers 7–2. He gives up six hits and a run, strikes out five, and doesn't walk anyone. He throws 124 pitches, going the distance for the Sox's first complete game of the season. In 1946,

Red Sox pitchers threw 79 complete games, second best among the eight American League teams.

The Sox are 26–12, holding an eight-game lead over the Yankees; they are nine games ahead of the Orioles, 9½ games in front of the Blue Jays, and 10 games ahead of the Devil Rays.

BOY, HE [MATSUZAKA] REALLY LOOKS LIKE THE REAL DEAL. The way he's handled himself and the way he pitches, he looks like he's been here the whole time. He really hasn't missed a beat. And it can't be easy for him. He's adjusting to so many new things. A new country, new language, new teammates, new league. But that might also be to his advantage. He's got so many pitches that he throws, the hitters don't know what to expect. And they're not familiar with him, so right now he's got the advantage. And he's got to take advantage of that. But I'll tell ya, he's fun to watch. I really like him.

You know, you hear a lot about pitch counts these days. We really didn't have pitch counts in my day. But I'm okay with pitch counts and things like that. I know a lot of the older guys think "just let them pitch." And I can see that, but I think pitchers are different now. They're used to pitching like this. It's exciting to see a complete game, especially if a guy has a really good game going. But you know, we have more pitching coaches, and trainers, and those people, but it seems like you see more pitchers getting injured now. No, I don't think you'll see any team getting that many complete games in a year ever again. You'd have to change the whole system so guys could get used to pitching that much. Pitch counts are okay. They kind of protect a young guy, but sometimes you do just want to let them go.

May 18, 2007

The Red Sox are hosting the Atlanta Braves for the start of interleague play. The first game is rained out, with a double-header scheduled for tomorrow.

I LIKE THE INTERLEAGUE GAMES. You get a look at the other league. I like that. I know I hear people saying they don't like playing the other league or maybe we've done it enough, it's time to stop. But I think it's kind of nice because if you get to the World Series, you're going to play a National League team. So now you get a little bit of a sneak preview. What do you think of the San Francisco Giants? I'm looking forward to seeing Barry Bonds. Then we get Colorado, Atlanta, San Diego, San Francisco, Arizona. It makes things interesting. And it's fun to see them play in the National League parks, playing the National League game. I know I'll see some players I haven't seen before and probably some guys I haven't even heard of before. It'll be fun.

May 19, 2007

Mike Lowell hits his sixth career grand slam in the fifth inning of the first game of a doubleheader (necessitated by rain the previous day) against the Braves at Fenway Park. In the twin bill, Lowell goes a combined 5-for-8, including 4-for-5 with two runs scored, a double, a grand slam, and five RBIs in the first game, as the Sox win 13–3. Lowell's performance helps Matsuzaka improve to 6–2—in his last three starts he is 3–0 with a 1.88 ERA.

The Sox split the doubleheader, taking the early game, 13–3, before dropping the nightcap 14–0. The Sox have won 10 of their last 13, and 17 of their last 23.

The Red Sox are 30–13, a .698 winning percentage. Maintaining their Major League–best record, they hold a 10½-game lead over both the Orioles and the Yankees, and they are 11 games ahead of the Blue Jays and 12 games ahead of the Devil Rays.

I LOVE MIKE LOWELL. The best way to describe him is he's a baseball player. I hope he stays here. I know he could go somewhere else next year, but I hope he stays here. He's just so solid. He does everything the way it's supposed to be done. On the field, at the plate, he just knows how things are supposed to be done. I remember him in spring training last year [in 2006] and I liked what I saw of him then. He's one of the best third basemen in the game today, and he's in a ballpark that's tailor-made for him. He's got power, but he also knows how to use that wall to bang doubles off it. When he gets in a little bit of a rut, he doesn't try to do too much. He just tries to meet the ball until he gets back on track. And he's such a nice guy. A great fielder. A fine arm. He just knows how to play. You don't have to worry about guys like him. You just put his name in the lineup and he goes out and plays and helps you win. Guys like that are great to have on a team, in a clubhouse, around younger guys. They just show how

Slugging third baseman Mike Lowell, a player that Johnny Pesky says "does everything the way it is supposed to be done."

things are supposed to be done without really saying anything. I call him "the senator." He just has such a dignity about him. And the way he plays, he reminds me a little of Frank Malzone. He's bigger than Malzone. But Malzone and Brooks Robinson were considered two of the best third basemen when they were playing. Lowell is not flashy. He just does the right things.

May 27, 2007

The Sox complete a three-game sweep of the Rangers in Texas, taking the series finale 6–5. The Sox take the difficult route in sweeping the Rangers in Arlington for the first time since August 20–22, 1973, coming from behind in each game.

Boston holds onto baseball's best record, 34–15 with a .694 winning percentage and an 11½ game lead over the Orioles, with the Blue Jays 12 back, the Yankees 12½ behind, and the Devil Rays 13½ back in the American League East.

Tomorrow is Memorial Day, which has Johnny reflecting on his years in the service and coming back to baseball when World War II ended.

OH, IT WAS REALLY A BREATH OF FRESH AIR. That's an expression, but it really was. Everything seemed different after that. It took a little time to get used to the goings-on. In other words, it was so good, you were so happy. It seemed like you didn't have to sleep very long to get back to the ballpark the next day. It was just wonderful to be able to come back and play baseball. It was like paradise. Everything just looked better. It felt better. It tasted better. It was just so good. I couldn't have been happier. To come back and see everyone…we had all made it back and we were together again. And we were playing baseball. It was just wonderful.

When the war was over, everybody was looking for points. They had a point system based on your service time, and I had just enough. I had a half point more than I needed. So I could get out. I was lucky. I got all my service time from the end of '42 to '46. I got my commission in '44. In '45 I was at Pearl Harbor, and the war ended while I was there. I was still on active duty. When I got enough points, they arranged transportation for us. I went to San Francisco. Then from San Francisco I took an aircraft up to Seattle and got discharged.

But it was wonderful to be able to go back and play baseball. I was 23 years old when I went into the navy and I was 26 when I got out. I hit a home run when I got back to Fenway, my first game after the war, on Opening Day. It was off Dick Fowler of the Athletics. We opened on the road, in Washington, but the Fenway opener was so special. Just to be back playing there, to have everyone back, it was something. Well, we beat the A's, 2–1; I scored both runs. The first I scored from second on an infield out, because I think they just forgot about me. Then I got the home run off Fowler in the eighth. But the play that I really like from that game was in the ninth. The A's had loaded the bases. One out, George Kell hit a ball up the middle. Bobby [Doerr] went over to get it, it took a weird bounce, hit him in the shoulder, and kind of came over to me. I just grabbed it, stepped on second base, threw to first. We got a double play, game over. Oh, what a great feeling it was. We were back in Boston. The war was over. We were playing baseball. And we won the game. What could be better?

May 28, 2007

Kevin Youkilis hits his first career inside-the-park home run as the Sox beat the Indians at Fenway, 5–3. After going 3-for-3 with two doubles, a walk, and a run scored, rookie second baseman Dustin Pedroia has his average up to .298. Starting the month hitting just .172, Pedroia has been feeling the heat from the Fenway Faithful, with many calling for him to be benched in favor of veteran Alex Cora. But Johnny likes what he has seen from the diminutive infielder.

HE'S VERY GOOD. He gets his hands dirty and he ain't afraid. I'm very proud of him. He's a much better player than I thought he was. I like what I saw when he first got here. Terry asked me to talk to him. I just watched him play a couple of days and I liked what I saw. His reactions were good.

I'm a little surprised. He's better than I thought. I thought he might struggle more than he has. He struggled a little bit at the beginning, but after that he really hasn't.

I like his aggressiveness. He's a dirt dog. He gets his hands dirty. He's a feisty little guy. He's one of those guys from the West Coast. He went to Arizona State. That's a good program out there, with Southern Cal, UCLA, Oregon, and Oregon State. They all have good programs. He's done very well. He's done every bit as good as I thought he would.

I'd say he's more like [White Sox Hall of Fame second baseman] Nellie Fox. He's a little scrappy guy. He's tough. Even his mannerisms are he wants to fight you. I like his makeup. I like his work habits. He's got excellent work habits. I'm not saying he's going to be a Bobby Doerr [the Red Sox's Hall of Fame second baseman]. They're two different bodies. But I'm very pleased with what he has done. He's a lot better player than I thought he

Rookie second baseman Dustin Pedroia surprised Johnny Pesky with his early-season performance: "He's better than I thought."

would be. But he's worked at it. He's a bulldog. The kind of kid you like. And he's always got a smile on his face.

I just think he was trying to do too much too fast. He was the number one draft pick, and he's a college kid. If he'd been in the minor leagues two more months, he wouldn't have had to go through that. But for a guy like that, you're better off when you go to spring training, getting the feeling of being with the big-league ballclub. There's a little bit to that. I didn't realize that until I got here. I had two years in the minor leagues and then I'm with the big-league ballclub and I'm put in the everyday lineup. I had guys like Doerr, Dom DiMaggio, Ted Williams, [Tex] Hughson, Dave Ferriss. The guys that were here, they had success. We sat in that corner over there and we talked a lot.

Of course Ted was the big guy, and he'd bark at you, and you wanted to please him. He'd talk and everybody else would listen. He commanded that respect. He was that way. A lot of people thought he was loud and boisterous, but he wasn't. He was the smartest guy I've ever been around, and he proved it. He was a fine guy. We had a good group, and they were all the same kinds of guys. We got along well because they played a little bit in the minor leagues together. Then they come here to the big club. It took a year to sort of get adjusted. Sometimes in those years it took you a little bit longer. These guys come in right away and make a hit, like Pedroia.

A four-game winning streak gives the Sox a 35–15 record with a .700 winning percentage, baseball's best record. The Sox have an 11½-game lead over the Orioles; they are 12 games ahead of the Blue Jays, with the Yankees and the Devil Rays 13½ games back.

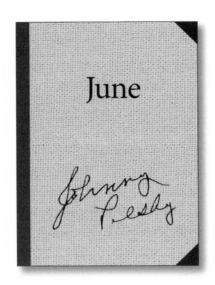

June

Johnny Pesky [signature]

June 1, 2007

The Sox host the Yankees for a three-game series at Fenway Park. Johnny has some guests visiting for the series. After losing Ruthie—his beloved wife of more than 60 years—almost two years ago, Johnny renewed acquaintances with a childhood friend, Evelyn, who is visiting from her home in Oregon with her three children and their spouses. It is the group's first visit to Fenway Park.

IT WAS VERY NICE. It was Evelyn, her three daughters, and their husbands. The Sox arranged to pick them up at the hotel and bring them to the ballpark. We fed them and we sat upstairs. Of course I had Evelyn sitting next to me. She had never been around stuff like that, but she got a kick out of it. And she was a little bit of a baseball fan when we were kids, so she had an idea.

When you're kids and you go your separate ways, you lose track of people. And then you hear about them and what they're doing. But my brother Vince kept in touch with Evelyn. She's very sweet. She was a great skater when we were kids. She was gorgeous. You couldn't get fresh with her, but I got really close to her and she to me. And she told me she was a little upset that we maybe only wrote one letter to one another and things stopped because I went to another part of the country and she was back going to school.

She was a golf enthusiast, and she met this fellow. They tell me he was a very nice guy. And she had all these kids and they just adore her. They were kidding her about Mama's got a boyfriend. Here we are, 60 years ago we dated quite a bit. We saw the Mills Brothers when they showed up. When I left Portland I went all the way to North Carolina to play baseball. Well, you know how that goes. You meet other people. The letters stop. You couldn't make phone calls back then. But now, I get a kick out of it because it's kind of childish. I'm 87 years old and you'd think I was 17, for chrissakes.

Oh, she loved being at Fenway. She thought it was great. She had fun. They took great care of her. She's very pleasant. She's got great skin. I don't know why I ever stopped writing to her. I guess I got busy playing ball. I got lazy. We used to skate together when we were kids.

I wasn't nervous having her at Fenway. Oh, no. I talk to her on the phone a lot.

The Sox's 9–5 loss to the Yankees puts a bit of a damper on the evening. Despite a two-game losing streak, the Sox hold baseball's best record, 36–17. The Orioles are 10 games back, the Blue Jays are 11½ games back, the Yankees are 12½ games out, and the Devil Rays are 13½ games behind in the division.

June 2, 2007

Kevin Youkilis's 23-game hitting streak—a career high that ties him for ninth-best in Red Sox history and second-best in baseball so far this season—comes to an end as the Sox beat the Yankees 11–6. The win ensures the Sox will avoid a three-game losing streak, which would have been their first of the season. In a scary moment in the seventh inning, Mike Lowell's leg hits the head of first baseman Doug Mientkiewicz, who was stretching for a catch. The blow seems to temporarily knock out Mientkiewicz.

The Sox are 37–17 with a .685 winning percentage. The Orioles are next in the American League East, 11 games back, with the Blue Jays 11½ games out, the Yankees 13½ games back, and the Devil Rays 14½ games behind.

YOUKILIS HAS REALLY WORKED HARD to make himself a good player. He's worked in the field and he's worked on his hitting. He's out there every day. You like a guy who will work like that. I think the longest streak I ever had was 12, 13 games. It's not

Hard-working first baseman Kevin Youkilis posted a 23-game hitting streak in early 2007 that was finally broken in the Red Sox's June 2 win over the Yankees.

easy. I never had one [a hitting streak as long as Youkilis's]. It's hard to do. When you're going good it looks easy, and you make it look easy to everybody else. But you go to bat three or four times a day. If you're a pretty good hitter, you get one out of four, or two out of four. That's if you're good, and lucky. A lot of times, if you get three out of four, you go 0-fer the next day.

That's baseball. That's how things happen. But you can't press to keep a streak going. And when you're going good, it doesn't feel like you're pressing. No, you just take it in stride because you know damn well someone's going to shut you out one of these days. A good hitter can hit .300, but that's only three hits in 10 times. So the pitchers have the advantage. Those pitchers are always watching. They look for some little thing they can find out about you.

Of course, I hit in front of the greatest hitter who ever lived [Ted Williams]. They never worried about me hitting the ball. They just said, "Here it is, you little bastard. Try and hit it." Dom [DiMaggio], me, Ted, Vern Stephens, then Bobby [Doerr]. We had good ballclubs, and we should have won two or three pennants. But we only won one. We should have won in '48, '49, and '50. But we didn't, because that's baseball and you just never can tell what's going to happen.

June 3, 2007

The Sox wrap up their weekend series with the Yankees, losing 6–5, dropping two games out of the three-game set.

Despite the loss, the Sox still have baseball's best record— 37–18 with a .673 winning percentage—and double-digit leads in the division, with the Blue Jays 10½ games behind, the Orioles 11 games back, the Yankees 12½ games out, and the Devil Rays 13½ games behind.

Today marks the 55th anniversary of the trade that sent Johnny with Walt Dropo, Fred Hatfield, Don Lenhardt, and Bill Wight to the Detroit Tigers for Dizzy Trout, George Kell, Johnny

Lipon, and Hoot Evers. The trade gave Pesky a front-row seat
for Al Kaline's debut the following season. Kaline would become
one of the best players in Tigers history.

I WAS AT HOME. I'd been with the ballclub six, seven years. That
wasn't uncommon. I'd gotten hurt and I wasn't as good as I could
have been. I kind of babied myself. I never dreamed I would get
traded. But I did, because in those days they traded guys like
us who still had time left in the game. I always said to [general
manager Joe] Cronin, "If you trade me, trade me to Detroit," and
he did. That was a big trade in '52.

I liked the city of Detroit, the ballpark. Old Tiger Stadium
was great. I could hit that ball in those seats. But my heart was
in Boston. Still, I wasn't disappointed. I was just getting over an
injury. I'd hurt my leg. I wasn't as good as I could have been. I
had a feeling I was going to get traded. [Walt] Dropo went in that
trade. Freddy Hatfield, Bill Wight, Don Lenhardt. There were
six of us. And they got Dizzy Trout, Hoot Evers, George Kell,
Johnny Lipon. It was a big trade. [Manager Lou] Boudreau came
in and he wanted to start from scratch, wanted the guys that he
thought he could win with.

But you see, when you have a good organization, you get a
chance. The Yankees were successful. The Tigers. The Cardinals.
The Cardinals had 30 teams. They had ballplayers coming out
of their ears, for god's sake. And you got along. A depression
was on in those years, and you were just looking to get a week's
pay. I was pretty lucky with what I was getting. My first year, I

was getting $150 a month. That was a lot of money. I had just turned 18. I was in Rocky Mount, North Carolina. The next year I was in Louisville; I was 19. Then when I got to the Red Sox, I thought I'd get sent back for sure. But I got there and I got a decent contract and I got a $5,000 bonus when that season was over. Then I went into the navy in 1942. Rocky Mount was 1940. Louisville was '41. Boston in '42. Then '43, '44, '45 I was in the navy. I came back and had a couple of pretty good years. In 1946 I had a great year. In the navy I lost three years, but we won the pennant in '46.

Joe Cronin became the general manager. He'd left the field. Steve O'Neill was the manager, but [Lou] Boudreau came over and he wanted to change the Red Sox. When I got traded I was at home on Western Avenue [in Lynn, Massachusetts]. I picked up the phone. It was Cronin. He said, "We just traded you to Detroit." [Walt] Dropo was living at my house at the time. Cronin said, "Is Dropo there? I want to talk to him." Dropo was out polishing his car in the driveway. I was having coffee with Ruthie. I said to Walt, "Cronin's on the phone. I think you're going to Detroit." So he said, "Oh, good." This was about 11:00 in the morning. We were on the train going to Philadelphia by 1:30. The Tigers were playing in Philly. So we got there pretty quick, and that was it. I started playing with Detroit.

I was so impressed when I first saw Kaline play. He was just an all-around great player. He had good size. He was right out of high school. I thought he was the best high school player I ever saw. He could run. He could throw. He had everything. When you get to watch a player like that starting out and then watching him develop into one of the best ever, it's very special. And he was such a nice person, too.

When I was with the Tigers, Fred Hutchinson [the legendary manager who died of cancer at the age of 45 in 1964, and for whom Major League Baseball's annual Hutch Award—given to an active player who best exemplifies a fighting spirit and the competitive desire to win—is named], who I'd known my whole life, he was the manager. He got the job just after I got there. I'd known him my whole life because he was from Seattle and I was from Portland. We were about the same age. I knew him from playing American Legion ball. Anyway, he wanted to keep me around. He said to Kaline, "When you're not playing"—Pat Mullin was the other old guy with me—"I want you to stay here and listen to these guys!" And what I would do is I'd have early workouts with these guys. Kaline, Reno Bertoia. Harvey Kuenn was in that group. A couple of others. We'd come out early and I'd get working out with them. So this was when I was still playing. But I was kind of acting like a coach, too, working with the kids. And I really enjoyed it. It got me thinking about what I wanted to do when I was done playing.

I could have stayed with them [the Tigers], because they wanted to give me a job. And I brought some new stuff into the organization. Then Detroit made changes and I came back to the Red Sox and I've been here ever since. A year with Washington. All but three years have been with Boston.

June 7, 2007

Curt Schilling has an incredible day, throwing a one-hit complete game—a 1–0 gem in Oakland—and stopping the Sox's four-game losing skid. Schilling gets two quick ground outs in the ninth before the A's Shannon Stewart steps to the plate. Schilling shakes off catcher Jason Varitek, then delivers a 95 mph fastball, his fastest of the game. Stewart sends a powerful line drive past second baseman Alex Cora into right field. "I've got the big 'what if' for the rest of my life," Schilling says after the game. Two pitches later, Cora gathers in Mark Ellis's pop foul to end the game. It would have been the first no-hitter of Schilling's 20-year big-league career.

Despite the recent skid, the Sox maintain baseball's best record, 38–21. Their lead in the division stands at 10 games over the Blue Jays, 10½ games over the Orioles and the Yankees, and 11½ games up on the Devil Rays.

HE [SCHILLING] SHOOK OFF THE CATCHER. Boy, I tell ya, I really wanted that for him. A no-hitter is so special for a pitcher. I tell you what, he's a helluva kid. He gets knocked around, he doesn't complain. He just says, "Well, I didn't have it today." He accepts responsibility. I hope they sign him for next year. He's the kind of guy who could be your 1-2-3 pitcher. I really think Schilling's got a couple of years left in him. It depends on what he wants to do. I hope he gets that no-hitter, though. He's come close a few times. That was just tough luck today.

But I really like our staff. You got the young guys. Right now [Josh] Beckett stands out like a sore thumb, he's so good. Beckett's a great pitcher. [Manny] Delcarmen I really like. [Jon] Lester is going to be good. Dice-K [Daisuke Matsuzaka] has been very good.

June 8, 2007

Major League Baseball's annual draft is underway. The Sox do not have a pick in the first round, making their first selection at number 55. They pick Nick Hagadone, a left-handed pitcher from the University of Washington. For the first time ever, the draft is being televised—just one more thing that's different from the way Johnny Pesky's decision to join the Boston Red Sox was made.

THE SCOUT FROM BOSTON, a guy named Ernie Johnson, would come in to watch me play and visit my house. My parents had a language barrier. They didn't understand the language. They were from Austria, Hungary, Croatia. My brother and sister went back to see the old countries, but I never did because I went away to play ball.

So anyway, scouts are coming around. The Red Sox guy came in. A guy from New York came in. The general manager from Cleveland came all the way to see me. The Detroit guy. The Cardinals. They were all coming in. My mother couldn't speak the language very well. So either my brother Tony or my sister Ann, who were the two oldest, would be there to help. My mother was easily embarrassed, so my brother and sister would say, "Ma, we'll take care of this." They'd talk to the scouts in English, and then translate to Croatian for my mother. My father was there, too, but he didn't care.

My mother's maiden name was Marja and my father was Jacob Paveskovich. My mother was embarrassed when I changed my name legally to Pesky. I said, "Ma, look, you're in America now. A lot of people do that." I told her about the radio programs she listened to. A lot of people on there changed their names. She asked me if I was ashamed of my name. I told her no. I said, "The kids call me that. Even when they come in the house, they call you Mrs. Pesky." So she got used to it. I was living up on Western Avenue in Lynn [Massachusetts] when I got it changed. But we had a good family. We were very Catholic.

My father didn't get involved with the scouts. My dad was a very nice man, very gentle. My mother was the disciplinarian. She had switches all over the house and she'd hit you on the butt with them. My sister Ann was the oldest, then Tony, Catherine, Millie, then me and Vinnie. Six of us—three boys, three girls. We call Vinnie "the Professor" because he went to college. That was something in those years.

Well, anyway, my mother liked the Red Sox scout that came to the house—Mr. Johnson. So every time the scout would come, he'd bring my father this bottle of bourbon. He'd sip it when he'd go to bed. It took him a month to drink a bottle. He'd just sip it, because my mother was always on him about it. But she really liked the Red Sox scout. He brought her beautiful flowers every time he came in. She really loved that. This went on for about three or four weeks. Then I had to make a decision.

I talked to my oldest brother, my sister, my mother and father. They wanted to be sure I got the right deal. Well, Ernie Johnson was very nice with my parents because he knew they had a language problem and that's really what won them over. He was a gentleman. He didn't try to get smart or pushy with them. And we got talking about, "Well, this is what the Tigers offered. This is what the Cardinals offered. This is what the Red Sox offered. This is what Cleveland offered." I had four offers. So naturally I wanted the most money, which was two grand. Well, the Red Sox offered $1,000. That was a lot of money back then. So I had to make a decision. Either that or I was going to go to school.

Well, I wasn't going to go to school! I said I wanted to pick the team that offered the most money. But my mother said, "No, pick Boston." She liked the scout. He brought those flowers and the bourbon for my dad—the other guys just showed up. She got to know him and she liked him. He was very nice to her and very patient. I told her I wanted the $2,000. I can still hear her like this, waggling her finger. She said, "Johnny, I don't care about the money, $2,000 to $1,000." She took the $1,000 because she liked the guy. She said, "This man will take care of you, Johnny."

So I signed with the Red Sox and went away to Rocky Mount, North Carolina. I had a good year. My manager wanted me to go to Boston. I was 18, 19 years old. I said, "No, I want to go home." I never did go. So I went from Class B Rocky Mount to Triple A Louisville, and I was the MVP of that league, and the next year I was with the Red Sox. Mother knows best. She was great. I was in Boston after two years of minor league ball. That was unheard of in those years. But that's how I ended up with the Red Sox, and I'm still with them after all these years.

The Sox beat the Diamondbacks, 10–3, in Arizona as J.D. Drew goes 3-for-5—including two three-run home runs—in a seven-RBI outing. Josh Beckett improves to 9–0, going eight innings and allowing three runs (two of them earned) on five hits without issuing a walk, striking out eight. The Sox improve to 39–21, with the Orioles and the Yankees 10½ games back, the Blue Jays 11 games out, and the Devil Rays 12½ games behind.

June 9, 2007

Shortstop Julio Lugo uses the hidden ball trick to tag out the Diamondbacks' unsuspecting Alberto Callaspo, who has strolled off second base. While Bill Coughlin, who played for the Senators and Tigers from 1901–08, is said to have pulled the trick a record seven times, no official records exist of that. It is believed Pesky managed the hidden ball trick three times in his career, a number that ties him with Marty Barrett—who was a master of the trick when he manned second base for the Sox in the 1980s—for most ever by a Red Sox player. Johnny's victims were Washington's Bill Zuber and the Yankees' Tommy Henrich in 1942, and Washington's Buddy Lewis in 1947. Lugo's successful use of the trick today is believed to be the 19th time in team history the Sox have pulled it off, going back to Candy LaChance, who caught Baltimore's Billy Gilbert on May 2, 1902. It was also the first time it has been used since Steve Lyons surprised the White Sox's Ozzie Guillen in the first inning during a game on May 13, 1991.

I PULLED THE HIDDEN-BALL TRICK THREE TIMES. The first one was on Bill Zuber and the second was on Tommy Henrich. We were playing in Boston. It was my rookie year. I knew about the hidden ball trick because someone had pulled it the year before. So we were playing and the umpires were watching closely. Henrich was on second base, and he turned to one of the umpires, Eddie Rommel. I got the ball from one of the outfielders. I put it in my glove. Henrich didn't know it because his back was to me. And I kind of walked a few steps towards him, and he said to the umpire, "Boudreau's been playing that hidden ball trick. This is as far as I'm going." And that was when I tagged him. The umpire started laughing. Henrich said, "You little bastard, I'll break your neck." But we were ahead by a few runs, and we won the game. Then I did it with the bases full another time.

Guys didn't really get too mad about the hidden-ball trick, though. You didn't really have to worry about getting plunked if you pulled it off. No, not really. They'd just throw me a fastball down the middle and let me get myself out. But I could handle a bat. If I could get my pitch, I could do something.

But the best trick I ever did wasn't the hidden-ball trick. I was the shortstop. [Vern] Stephens was playing third. We were playing St. Louis. Mel Parnell was the pitcher. Stephens has a bunch of assists. It was the bottom of the ninth and we were leading by a bunch of runs [the Sox would eventually win 12–0]. Lou Boudreau was playing shortstop, but he went out of the game and I took his place at short. I played the ninth. I said to Stephie [Stephens]—we were talking about this in the dug-

Red Sox shortstop Julio Lugo pulled off an unlikely hidden-ball trick on June 9 when he tagged out the Diamondbacks' Alberto Callaspo, who was leading off second base.

out—I said, "Roomie, if the ball's hit to me, you got to be careful, be ready." And he thought I was kidding. So Ken Wood, a big outfielder with St. Louis, he hit a ground ball right to me. I caught the ball. Stephens was over there. I threw him the ball and he threw the ball to first and threw Wood out. That's how he got the record for assists. [Stephens holds the Sox's record for assists by third basemen in a single game with 10, a feat he achieved on May 23, 1951; the record was later tied by Frank Malzone.] Stephie's eyes, I thought they were going to bug out. He didn't think I was going to do it. But the ball was hit so hard, if it was in the hole, I couldn't do it. Everybody in the stands thought I was crazy until they figured out what was going on. I came out a hero. We had a good lead so it was okay. I think it went a guy flied out, then somebody popped up. Nobody on base, two outs, and the ball's hit sharply to me. I just flipped it to him. He got rid of the ball like it was on fire. That's something that you very rarely see. I went to an affair that night, with the gridiron club, I think. It was the topic of the day. It was fun.

The Sox beat Arizona 4–3 on Mike Lowell's pinch-hit sacrifice fly in the tenth inning, giving the Sox a three-game winning streak. The Sox are 40–21 with a .656 winning percentage. The Yankees are 10½ games back, with the Blue Jays 11 games out, the Orioles trailing by 11½ games, and the Devil Rays with a 12½-game deficit.

June 11, 2007

After taking the first two games in Arizona, the Sox lose 5–1 and face 12 consecutive games against teams from the senior circuit. The Rockies will visit Fenway Park for three games before the Giants return to the lyric little bandbox for the first time since the *New York* Giants came for the 1912 World Series. The Giants also played the Boston Braves in the regular season at Fenway, with the last matches taking place June 1–3, 1915. Later the Sox and the Giants played several exhibition games in Boston to benefit the Jimmy Fund. The last two contests are believed to have been played August 16, 1954, and May 23, 1955. In the '55 game, Ted Williams homered and Norm Zauchin homered *twice* in a 4–3 Sox victory. The Giants' last regular-season game in Boston was on September 1, 1952, when the New York Giants split a doubleheader with the Boston Braves at Braves Field.

With the Giants' appearance, the only National League team that has not played at Fenway Park since the inception of interleague play is the Chicago Cubs. After the series with the Giants, the Sox will travel to Atlanta and San Diego for their final games against National League teams this year—unless the Sox have a World Series appearance in their future this season, that is.

Sox fans of a certain age remember a time when the Sox didn't have to travel beyond the city limits to face a National League team.

THAT WAS FUN WHEN THE BRAVES WERE HERE. I really enjoyed that. They played when we were on the road, and we were at home when they were on the road. If you were a baseball fan, you could go to a game in Boston just about any day you ever wanted. What could be better than that? We followed the Braves. We had friends over there. Johnny Sain, Warren Spahn, Earl Torgeson. We'd play them in the spring. We had a city series, just like we have now with the Twins in Fort Myers in the spring.

They had some great pitching over there, Sain and Spahn. They had Lew Burdette. He was a cheater, though, he always spit on the ball. They had Bobby Hogue, Johnny Antonelli, the left-hander. And then, you know, you look at the Braves now over the last few years, and they've had great pitching again. [John] Smoltz, [Tom] Glavine, [Greg] Maddux. The Braves always had great pitching back in the day.

That's what makes interleague play fun. You see someone you haven't even heard of before, and it really opens your eyes. And if you're a hitter, you want to see as many pitchers like that as you can. It makes you a better hitter. Even if you don't face them, you can sit and watch and study them. You watch, when a team comes in that they haven't seen before, they're all sitting in the dugout watching. Years ago they used to warm up in front of the dugouts. I remember watching [Bob] Feller warm up. I'd be thinking, "Oh, Jesus, not him today."

I don't know if I could say who was the toughest pitcher I ever faced. Well, there was certainly more than one. We had some tough pitching back then. I remember there was a guy with the old St. Louis Browns by the name of Frank Biscan. Geez, he couldn't break an egg, but all he did was throw the ball up there and he got me out so easy. But I liked guys who threw hard. Not 100 mph, like [Bob] Feller, [Bob] Gibson, [Virgil] Trucks, [Dizzy] Trout, [Hal] Newhouser. When Detroit had Trucks, Newhouser, and Trout all going at the same time, the papers used to call them TNT. And you know, they were right!

Oh, geez, we had some tough pitchers then. You went into Washington, they had [Ray] Scarborough, [Walt] Masterson, [Sid] Hudson. Jesus, then you go up to Philadelphia, they had [Lou] Brissie, [Dick] Fowler. Go out to Chicago, they had Ted Lyons, Eddie Lopat. Then go to New York, you've got Whitey Ford, Don Larsen. There wasn't much of a break anywhere.

June 12, 2007

Today the Sox open a three-game series with the Colorado Rockies, who bring Todd Helton with them. Helton made a run at hitting .400 in 2000, reaching that exact milestone several times that season, including on August 21. He became the first player to reach that vaunted mark that late in a season in 20 years; before him, the last player to achieve such a feat was George Brett, who did so on September 4, 1980. Helton finished 2000 hitting .372. Brett ended 1980 at .390.

I JUST DON'T KNOW IF WE'LL EVER SEE THAT AGAIN. There are so many things that have to go right. And you have to have the right player for it. I don't know. It would have to be a guy like [Ted] Williams who could hit home runs too. But see, Williams didn't strike out much. He had great vision, tremendous hand-eye coordination. We had a lot of good hitters.

Luke Appling was a good hitter with the White Sox. He led the league in hitting. They had a lot of good players over there in Chicago. There was Cecil Travis and Mickey Vernon with Washington. You had Bob Dillinger and Vern Stephens with the

Browns. Then you went to Detroit and they had good hitters the years we played. Kaline came along in '53.

They had a great team. Virgil Trucks, Dizzy Trout, Hal Newhouser. Hank Greenberg was gone to Pittsburgh. Harvey Kuenn the shortstop, Frank Bolling. Detroit had some good players. Detroit, New York, Boston at that time had some great players. Yet you look at all of them, and none of them hit .400.

You take all the great players of baseball history—Joe DiMaggio, Ted Williams, Bobby Doerr, and all the other good players. You categorize them. But then you have your superstars. Al Kaline: superstar. Joe DiMaggio: superstar. Hank Greenberg: superstar. Guys like that. They were all big, strong guys with tremendous ability. And there's a lot of guys our size who are outstanding players and they just fit a need. Like, if you're a middle infielder, you've got to be able to run. You've got to be able to catch the ball. Your job is to set up an inning for the heavy hitters, the three, four, five, six hitters. And that's the way it works. If your one and two guys get on base, it makes it easier for the guys coming up behind them to do their jobs.

Dominic [DiMaggio] and I, we got along so well, and for a number of years we scored over 100 runs each. That's a lot of runs. And Williams wasn't going to get a hit every time, but he produced more than he didn't. He was successful more than he was unsuccessful. He was the last guy to hit over .400.

Every couple of years you'll see a guy make a run at hitting .400. They get part way into the season and they're still really hitting the ball. But it's such a long season. You get tired late in the season. Your body starts to wear down. Or you might start pressuring yourself. Or the fans want so much from you. You might start pressing for them. And the media wants to know all about it. You might be asked to do a lot of interviews. It's just not easy. It's such a hard thing to do. Ted always said the hardest thing to do is hit a round ball with a round bat. But he did it better than anybody. I don't know. It's fun to watch guys when they're hitting close to .400, to see how they're doing. But I don't know if we'll ever see anyone hit .400 again. But if someone does, I hope I'm around for it.

The Sox beat the Rockies 2–1 on a J.D. Drew eighth-inning sacrifice fly, giving Tim Wakefield (6–7, 3.92 ERA) his first win at Fenway Park since April, with Jonathan Papelbon picking up his 15th save. Despite the win the Sox are only 5–5 in their last 10 games, but at 41–22, with a .651 winning percentage, they still hold baseball's best record. Their lead in the division is 9½ games over the Yankees, 11½ games over the Blue Jays and the Devil Rays, and 12½ games over the Orioles.

June 14, 2007

The Sox lose to the Rockies at Fenway Park, 7–1, dropping two out of three to Colorado. Catcher Jason Varitek goes 2-for-4, giving him 1,000 hits in his career. The switch-hitting Varitek, hitting .275, is always a valuable asset in the middle of the lineup. But his primary value is not at the plate—it's behind the plate.

HE'S AN EXCELLENT CATCHER. One of the best in the game, probably the best. He could be a better hitter, but I think he's trying so hard, and he's so important to the pitchers. It's not an easy job for him. But he is so important to this club. You look back at some catchers—Johnny Bench, Bill Dickey, Mickey Cochrane, Gabby Hartnett. Well, all those guys put the ball in play. Jason just has to watch the ball. He's a big, strong guy. You expect him to hit home runs. You don't expect him to hit .330, but you expect him to hit .260 to .280, because he's that kind of hitter. And late in the ballgame, as the pitcher, you're used to seeing a guy. And right now, you get so many different pitchers coming into a ballgame, you get so many different looks, the pitchers get the advantage. But he's got a fine line, because he's so important to our pitching staff and he puts so much work into that. He is so valuable to this team.

I really think Carlton Fisk is the best catcher we ever had here. That's an easy one. I don't even have to think about it. He's in the Hall of Fame. That makes it easy for me to decide. It's nice to see him come back to the park once in a while now. He's up in that Legends' Suite once in a while, like I am. He's a great kid. I ran into him and his wife the other day, and they were so nice to me.

Birdie Tebbetts might have been the best I played with. He put the ball in play. He was a little pepper pot. He didn't strike out very much. He didn't have much power, but he was Phi Beta Kappa, a college boy. He went to Providence College. Nice guy. He was with Detroit all those years, and we got him in '47, and he helped us. He was a smart guy, a typical catcher. He handled pitchers pretty well. He'd bark at them, and you couldn't get mad at him. He had that Irish look. He was a great guy.

A good catcher really knows how to work with his pitchers. Yogi Berra was no Phi Beta Kappa, but he could catch and he could throw. He must have been taught by somebody, maybe Bill Dickey, because they were both great. Yogi was a pure hitter and a great guy, and he was on five straight world championship teams.

When you get guys like Varitek and Fisk, they are so valuable to a team—behind the plate, in the clubhouse, the way the go about their business. They're workers. No nonsense. They just do things right. It's good to have guys like that on your team. I love it.

The Sox loss gives them a season record at 41–24. The Yankees are in second place in the American League East, 7½ games back, with the Blue Jays 10 games behind, the Devil Rays 11½ games out, and the Orioles 12½ games behind.

June 22, 2007

The Sox place Curt Schilling on the disabled list today with right shoulder tendinitis. Since throwing a complete-game, one-hit victory in Oakland on June 7, the 40-year-old Schilling has gone a total of only 9.1 innings in his last two starts, allowing a combined 11 earned runs on 19 hits—including two home runs, three walks, and five strikeouts.

The Sox win in San Diego, 2–1, as Dice-K Matsuzaka improves to 9–5 with a 4.01 ERA while besting the Padres' Greg Maddux.

The Sox are 47–25, maintaining the best record in baseball. The Yankees are 10½ games back, with the Blue Jays 12 games behind, and the Orioles and the Devil Rays 15½ games out.

WE'RE ALWAYS BETTER WITH SCHILLING IN THE ROTATION. But I'm not worried. I know he'll be back soon. Everyone talks about how old he is, 40. But he's got a good body. He's strong. He takes care of himself. There are a lot of guys who get late in their lives and they're better pitchers. They start to actually pitch instead of just relying on their strength. I think Schilling could be like that. He could pitch for the next two or three years, if he wants to. I imagine when he can't do what he thinks he should do, he'll just retire. But I hope he stays in baseball in some capacity. I think he's a wonderful young man, first, and he's a wonderful player. He's so family oriented. I get along great with him. He calls me a little weasel. I call him a big turd, but it's all in fun. He's a wonderful kid. When he first came here and he got that big contract, he gave a million dollars to the Jimmy Fund. I like to watch him pitch. I don't like to see him struggle, but he adjusts to it. If someone gets a base hit off him, he doesn't stomp around the mound. He just gets the ball and says, "Okay, I'll get the next guy." I always watch the look on his face because he's so darned dedicated to what he wants to do, and it's wonderful. I hope he can pitch for another couple of years. I know he has enough sense so that when he feels he can't do it, he'll get out. But I just want him to come back healthy and strong this year. We need him on the mound.

June 28, 2007

An off day for the Sox, who return from a six-game trip through San Diego and Seattle, going 2–4 on the trip—2–1 in San Diego, 0–3 in Seattle. Despite the disappointing road trip, the Sox hold a 9½-game lead over the second-place Blue Jays. They are 10½ games ahead of the Yankees, 14½ games over the Orioles, and 15 games ahead of the Devil Rays. At 48–29, with a .623 winning percentage, they still hold baseball's best record.

WELL, I DIDN'T LIKE THE TRIP, THE LAST COUPLE OF DAYS. They shouldn't lose them like they did. They had every chance to win two of those ballgames, but that's going to happen. You can't expect every day the guy who's supposed to do it will do it. It isn't always going to happen. But we have a nine-game lead, for god's sake. You'd think, for god's sake, we were in the outhouse. We had a bad time, but the Yankees haven't even picked up a game on us in two weeks. They had every chance. If they'd have won four or five games, they'd be about four or five back. You could make that up in four or five days. That's how quick this thing can change.

We have a good team. I think it's every bit as good as last year's. I think the pitching is better. I like the pitching very much. [Josh] Beckett's been great. [Julian] Tavarez has pitched well, which I was glad for. I always liked Tavarez, and he's done pretty well. Of course, you expect Schilling to be good. I just hope he's all right. I hope he's not physically hurt. He's in his forties, but he's one of those tough guys. The thing I like about him, he doesn't spit the bit. I like his makeup. I always have. He had that as a kid. He should have never left here. But he's traveled and he's been successful every place he's ever been. He's been a winner. He's got a fine arm.

He reacts to Fenway. He loves it here. Of course, the fans here are great. Every pitch he throws, they're oohing and aahing, and this is something you don't get a lot of places, even at the major league level. When you have a full house every day, they kind of make a lot of noise. And that makes a big difference.

June 30, 2007

Jacoby Ellsbury, one of the most exciting players in the Red Sox's minor league system, makes his debut tonight at Fenway Park against the Rangers. Ellsbury goes 1-for-4, starting in center field, as the Sox lose to the Rangers, 5–4. Josh Beckett falls to 11–2 with a 3.38 ERA.

The Sox are 49–30 with a 10½-game lead over the Blue Jays and the Yankees, a 14½-game lead over the Orioles, and a 16-game edge on the Devil Rays.

Johnny has a special affinity for Ellsbury, another of Oregon's native sons.

I LIKE HIM. I LIKE HIM VERY MUCH. Boy, can he run. So far I really like him. He's got a nice, level swing. He's not trying to do too much. He's a good-sized kid. He's not a big kid, but he looks like he's got good judgment. But, oh, he can run. God, he can fly!

I haven't talked to him too much today. I talked to him in spring training. I met his family. I don't want to say too much.

One of Johnny's favorite young players is outfielder Jacoby Ellsbury (like Pesky, an Oregon native), who made his Fenway Park debut on June 30.

He's going to be busy today. It's nice to see guys like that. I like to see guys play. Sometimes you hear about a guy in the minors and then they get up here and can't do anything. But he looks pretty good.

I was very impressed. It looks like he's a good outfielder. I was very impressed with his speed. I like the way he swings—nice and level.

It's fun to see young guy come up for the first time. Oh, yeah. They're excited, and they're trying so hard to impress. But if you just be yourself, after you're around a while, then you'll find out what kind of a player you are. Guys will kid you, but they don't kid young players anymore as much as they used to.

I was hitting .330 in the minor leagues. I thought I was a hotshot. Then I got up here and there were guys who had played the game for years and they looked at you as if to say, "What are you doing here?" But it was all in fun. And the thing is, when we got here, when we got to the Red Sox, we had Ted Williams, Bobby Doerr. We had Dom DiMaggio. Great players. We had a good team, good pitching.

It's funny how players make an impression with you. Sometimes you like a guy and sometimes you don't. You might like him, but he's got to be better. So you hit in the minor leagues? Well, let's see what you do in the big leagues where the pitching is better, the fielding is better, the hitting is better, they throw that at you. Well, you better be able to overcome that. If you're a good player, you'll get in the mix of things. Just keep your mouth shut and go. You take most of the good players—Bobby Doerr was very quiet. Dominic, Christ, you had to pull his teeth to get him to talk. Tex Hughson never stopped talking. Dave Ferriss was very quiet. Mickey Harris, well, he could talk a dog off a meat wagon. We had a lot of good guys.

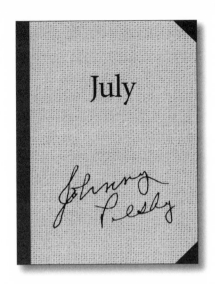

July 2, 2007

The Sox pound out 10 hits in their 7–3 win over the Rangers at Fenway as Eric Hinske goes 2-for-4 with three RBIs and a run scored, and Kason Gabbard (2–0, 5.79 ERA) picks up the win.

The Sox are 50–31 with a .617 winning percentage—good for first place in the American League East—but they are no longer in possession of baseball's best record. That distinction goes to the Angels, who have a record of 51–31 with a .622 winning percentage. The Sox still have a healthy lead in the division, however, with the Blue Jays and the Yankees 10½ games back, the Orioles 14½ games out, and the Devil Rays 17 games behind.

Jacoby Ellsbury shows off his speed when he scores from second on a wild pitch in the fourth inning.

I NEVER SAW THAT BEFORE. I've seen guys score from third base, of course, but never one from second base. I said that to him the other day. I call him "Ellzie." I told him I've been in the game my whole life and I've never seen that before. That was something. He's a nice kid. He just says, "Oh, really?" I told him to just keep it up. He can run, I'll tell ya. Boy, he's fast! I heard about him a couple of years ago when I was home. I met him at a dinner two years ago. Since he got here, I haven't spent much time with him, but I enjoy watching him.

Another guy I've enjoyed watching is that little second base-man, [Dustin] Pedroia. They've got a bunch of exciting kids. But the young players do that. They come up and they can energize a team and the fans.

July 5, 2007

Prior to the sixth inning, the giant scoreboard above Fenway's center field announces that reliever Hideki Okajima has been added to the American League All-Star team, prompting an unprecedented round of bows to every corner of the park from the Japanese pitcher.

THAT WAS GREAT TO SEE. I think he belongs there. Of course, [Jonathan] Papelbon was going to go.

Right now this ballclub is fantastic. It doesn't have a weakness. They're all worried about [Julio] Lugo. Lugo's a fine player. He's going to come around. He's not hitting right now, but he will. And he's a fine shortstop. And they're winning. But this kid has a reputation of being a throwback from the old school. Like Joe Cronin [a seven-time All-Star shortstop for the Senators and the Red Sox], Cecil Travis [an All-Star shortstop/third baseman for the Senators], and Harvey Kuenn [an eight-time All-Star with the Tigers and Indians]. He's a tall, skinny kid, but he can run. Right now he catches everything that's hit to him. I think he's a fine player, and he's going to come around.

Josh Beckett improves to 12–2 with a 3.44 ERA as the Sox sweep the Devil Rays, pounding out 21 hits in the 15–4 series finale. Mike Lowell and Coco Crisp each have five RBIs, with Crisp delivering a first-inning grand slam.

At 53–31, the Sox are once again in possession of baseball's best record, with a .631 winning percentage. The Yankees are 11½ games back, while the Blue Jays are 12 games behind, the Orioles are 16½ games out, and the Devil Rays are 20 games back. The Sox head to Detroit for a three-game series next, closing out the first half of the season.

WHEN YOU'RE ON THE WINNING SIDE of a blowout like that, it's great. It gives you a chance to get a couple of extra hits. As a manager, you shouldn't have to worry about keeping guys focused. You take that in stride. When you have so many games, you dissect. In your own mind, you want to win today because tomorrow might never come. It might rain tomorrow. So you worry about today and you play your best players and that's really all you can do. Terry Francona is a very good manager. He doesn't have to worry about keeping his players focused.

"Terry Francona is a very good manager" is Johnny Pesky's simple assessment of the Boston skipper, shown here congratulating Hideki Okajima. "He doesn't have to worry about keeping his players focused."

I'll tell you who was a good manager and never got credit—Don Zimmer. I thought Don Zimmer knew the game. Ralph Houk knew the game. All those guys, they study certain things. One thing about baseball, you can get too smart. Just maintain your stability. And if the ownership is with you, that's even better.

Right now Terry's in a great place. There're some things that he does that I'm not going to second-guess him about. He knows what he wants, but sometimes that doesn't work. But he's a good manager and he's good with people.

Now, when you're on the losing side of those kinds of games, it's purgatory. It's tough. Or when you're losing a bunch in a row, it's bad. The old St. Louis Browns had that problem. When I was playing, you'd watch them struggle and feel for them, and the Philadelphia A's. And they got better. All those teams, you improve with talent. The only way you're going to improve is with talent because people don't like to come out and watch a losing team. It's a cycle. If you have better talent, more people come out, and the more people come out, the better players you can get.

This should be a good series this weekend in Detroit. They have a very good team right now. I was glad to see them do so well last year. I don't want to see them beat us, but I was glad to see them do well. I think they're a tough team. They've got good pitching. They've got some good young hitters. They're going to be tough. Luckily, we won't have to face that young [Justin] Verlander. Phew! He's tough!

July 8, 2007

The Sox lose to the Tigers, 6–5, closing out the first half of the season with a disappointing three-game series loss in Detroit. The Tigers are a game ahead of the Indians in the American League Central. Daisuke Matsuzaka falls to 10–6 with a 3.84

ERA. In five innings, he allows six runs on 10 hits and a walk, while striking out four.

The Sox end the first half of the season with a 53–34 record and a .609 winning percentage, baseball's best. The Yankees are 9½ games back, in second place, followed by the Blue Jays 10 games out, the Orioles 15½ games back, and the Devil Rays 19 games behind.

RIGHT NOW, I THINK THE TIGERS are the biggest threat in the league. They've improved their ballclub. They've moved people in. Gary Sheffield is always a threat. They've got [Magglio] Ordonez. Their young pitching is tremendous. Especially that Justin Verlander. We didn't have to face him this weekend. That's a good thing. Jim Leyland brought a big change. He's a fine man. He came out of the National League. He's a no-nonsense guy. He's got the personality to go with it. He's a wonderful man. You can talk to him. He's not an ego guy. He's like an Al Lopez or a Ralph Houk. He commands respect. A lot of people think because you're in charge, you have to be a certain way. It doesn't always work that way when you're dealing with the human element. It takes a lot of courage. You try to surround yourself with good people, your coaches especially. People you can work with. And this is what Terry's done. Brad Mills is probably the best coach I ever saw. I've been in the game my whole life. If I had to pick one guy, it would be Brad Mills. They know each other. They've been together a long time. They became good friends. They understand the game.

Detroit has always been one of my favorite ballclubs. I was glad to see them turn it around. Right now their scouting is every bit as good as anyone's. The Red Sox have good scouts. The Yankees always had good scouts. The years that we played, the scouts were right there every day watching the players. They wanted to make sure there wasn't a mistake going to be made if they signed a guy. I got $1,000 to sign and $150 a month. That was 1940, when I started. I went to Class B. I gave my signing bonus to my parents, and the Red Sox bought the house for my parents. I think the house cost $5,000. Mr. Yawkey [Tom Yawkey, owner of the Sox from 1933 until his death in 1976] gave me a bonus when I got to Boston. A $5,000 bonus, and I gave that to my parents. Everything went to them. And then I went into the navy. When I got back, I depended on my throwing ability. I was never a $100,000 ballplayer. But [Ted] Williams and [Joe] DiMaggio, your great players, could command that. When you can command that, you're a pretty good guy. I thought Ted Williams was the smartest player ever, and Joe DiMaggio. We had some guys on our ballclub who were great players

Ted Williams, Tex Hughson, Bobby Doerr, Dom DiMaggio. These are players that I considered family. I think it was much nicer when we played. You didn't have all this crap going on. Our big thing was to win today. If we didn't win today, we wanted to win tomorrow and the next game and next week. Try to win as many games as you possibly could and your gift would be to get into the playoffs and the World Series. That's the way it was in the years we played. Now it's different. Now these guys are making a lot of money. Some of them look like they don't care. You don't see as much emotion as we did. But they do care. Some of them do. The guy that probably does the most on the ballclub is Papi [David Ortiz].

When Nomar [Garciaparra] was here, I thought he was going to take the place of a Joe Cronin because of his playing abilities. And he had a quietness to him. I thought Garciaparra was one of the best players we ever had here. I say that to this day. He was hitting .300, 30 home runs, All-Star shortstop every year, and then as the season went on he was hurt and getting older and the club felt they had to make a deal. But he's still playing.

We didn't end the first half [of the season] on a good note, but I'm not worried. We'll take a little break here, and come back after the All-Star Game. I'm looking forward to the second half.

July 10, 2007

The All-Star Game is tonight, and the Red Sox are well represented by David Ortiz, Mike Lowell, Josh Beckett, Jonathan Papelbon, Manny Ramirez, and Hideki Okajima on the American League squad. The Red Sox are coming off a three-game sweep by the Tigers in Detroit. Their lead over the Yankees is down to 9½ games. Johnny Pesky is having breakfast with his regular crew at the Salem Diner.

I WATCHED THE HOME-RUN HITTING CONTEST LAST NIGHT. That's fun, but our guys weren't in it. I'm going to watch the game

Boston designated hitter David "Big Papi" Ortiz was one of six Red Sox players named to the 2007 American League All-Star team. The AL downed the NL 5–4 for their fifth straight victory in the contest.

tonight. I love the All-Star Game. I look forward to it. We've got enough of our guys in there to make it fun. We're pretty well represented—Papi [David Ortiz], [Josh] Beckett, [Jonathan] Papelbon, Manny [Ramirez], [Mike] Lowell, [Hideki] Okajima. I went a couple of times. I was on the coattails of those other guys—Ted [Williams], Bobby [Doerr]. It's so much different now. It's a wonderful thing to go. You get a nice gift. We got pretty nice rings one year. But it's just such an honor.

Some people think the All-Star Game has lost some of its luster. But no, no, I don't think so. It's very satisfying when you get picked. It's a helluva thrill. I was in two of them, as a player and as a coach. When Ralph Houk was managing, I came over here and I worked for him. Coaching with a good big-league ballclub is great. The Yankees, Red Sox, Detroit, and I thought Pittsburgh at that time were good. Detroit was always good, and I think they're back to where they were. Jim Leyland is probably one of the best guys you ever want to meet. He's a throwback from old-time baseball. Terry is a little bit like that too. He's a philosopher; he's got his own opinions.

Detroit gave us a tough time this weekend. Well, that can happen. They're a very good team. And it's great to see them back like that. The Yankees are the ones that are really in a bind, and they've got a helluva ballclub. If they were to start the season tomorrow, you'd take the Yankees. They've got A-Rod [Alex Rodriguez], [Derek] Jeter, [Hideki] Matsui. You know who's not having a good year is [Johnny] Damon. He's had some injuries. [Jorge] Posada is doing well, but their pitching has been very suspect. But [Roger] Clemens is still Clemens. They've had a tough time so far this year. But they're still the Yankees. You've got to watch out for them.

I still like us, though. We're in first place. But like every team, we get into a little bit of a valley. We're in a little bit of a valley now.

Everybody's saying things. We got swept in Detroit but we're still 9½ games up. These other teams have to play each other. It's the teams behind you that have to put things together.

July 11, 2007

The American League won last night's All-Star Game, its fifth consecutive win in the Midsummer Classic. The AL has won every All-Star Game since it was decided that the winning league would receive the home-field advantage in the following World Series. Johnny Pesky was selected for All-Star Games as both a player and a coach, and was the starting shortstop in 1946, his first season back after three years in the navy.

WELL, I WAS IN A COUPLE. They picked guys for a position. But I played with some guys, like [Dom] DiMaggio [who played in six All-Star Games] and [Ted] Williams [18], Mickey Vernon [seven]. We didn't have as many teams then, but we played a lot of games. I think the atmosphere was much tougher. You had to be pretty good to make the All-Star team. I know there were a couple of years when we had guys that hit pretty well and didn't make it, and they asked why they didn't, and they were told, "Well, we needed a guy for a certain job. We can't have two of them."

You felt pretty good to get picked. We had a lot of good shortstops in the American League. We had Phil Rizzuto. Cecil Travis was at Washington. I was at Boston. Who was at Detroit? It might have been Johnny Lipon at that time, and then Harvey Kuenn.

But there were a lot of good players at that time, and some of them didn't make it. And that's always a problem.

I think when they get the fans involved and a guy gets a lot of votes, he should go. It's a privilege to play in the All-Star Game, I think. Years ago, the writers used to pick the All-Star teams, and you had to be a pretty good player for the writers to pick you because they were more concerned about the players as individuals. There's so much now about favorites.

I'm not surprised that Manny [Ramirez] went and [David] Ortiz. [Jason] Varitek didn't get picked, but he should have. [Josh] Beckett, right now he's one of the best pitchers in the game. He and [Curt] Schilling are a great combination. I hope Schilling will be all right. We need him. [Kevin] Youkilis definitely should have gone. He's hitting .330. He's really come on in the last six weeks. He's driven in a lot of runs. He's been a very good hitter. He's the kind of hitter I thought he was going to be when he was a kid—a line-drive type of hitter. I like those kinds of guys who are strong. They can hit a home run. Most good hitters have that nice, level swing. They swing through the ball. Ted Williams said, "Hit a strike. If you don't hit a strike, you ain't gonna hit."

The All-Star Game is a spectacle. It's supposed to be like that. I would like to have one in each league. That way the Red Sox could send Ortiz and Youkilis, instead of choosing one over the other.

I like the All-Star Game very much. Years ago you didn't see the other league. You had to do it the hard way, by going to the World Series, and they had all those great pitchers in the National League—[Sandy] Koufax, [Don] Drysdale, [Johnny] Vander Meer with Cincinnati.

July 12, 2007

The Red Sox open the second half of the season at home against the Blue Jays, who are in third place in the American League East, 10 games back. The Red Sox are 53–34, with a .609 winning percentage, just ahead of the Tigers (at 52–34, .605) for the best record in baseball. The July 31 trade deadline is less than three weeks away.

I'M LOOKING FORWARD TO THE SECOND HALF [of the season]. I think we have a good team. We're in the driver's seat right now.

I'd have to say just leave the team right where it is. I was hoping they'd keep [Jacoby] Ellsbury up, but that's just a personal thing for me. I don't think Wily Mo [Pena] is the answer. If he was playing in our day, he'd be back in Triple A, and we'd let him stay there and play every day and let him work on things. He's got a lot of potential and he's a helluva nice kid, but he needs work. He needs to play every day. He needs to be able to work on things. But he's a nice kid and he's willing to work, and that's a good thing. That's very important. But he needs to play. And we have so many good outfielders ahead of him here, he's just not going to get enough playing time.

I think it's a good ballclub. Right now, we're in a good position. All they have to do is play .500 the rest of the year, and they'll be in the World Series.

July 19, 2007

The Red Sox are in the middle of a four-game series with the White Sox at Fenway, Chicago's only trip to Fenway this year. The Red Sox lose to the White Sox, 4–2, as Daisuke Matsuzaka allows three runs and two hits in five innings. He struggles with control in the loss, walking six (though also striking out six) and dropping his record to 11–7 with a 3.99 ERA.

With a record of 56–39, the Red Sox are no longer in possession of baseball's best record. They are only 20–23 since June 1. Their lead in the AL East is down to 6½ games, with the Yankees in second place, followed by the Blue Jays at 10 games back, the Orioles 14 games out, and the Devil Rays 18½ games behind. The Sox have lost three games in a row and have had only three wins in their last 10 games. The Yankees, meanwhile, are one of the hottest teams in baseball.

I'M NOT REALLY WORRIED. Well, of course things could happen. But there'll be some changes made, I'm sure, because that's what happens. Because you can't let this get into a long slumber. Right now, I think the ballclub is really sound. The pitching's been good. Our offense could be better, I think. [David] Ortiz hasn't been hitting like he was. And Manny [Ramirez] isn't hitting like he can. I think they're a little disappointed in a couple of guys, but it's always that way.

But the guy who's picked up is the shortstop [Julio Lugo]. He's doing very, very well. He's doing some hitting and he's one of the better players lately. He certainly can do better than he's been hitting. But that happens. You hit valleys like this as a hitter. Ted Williams never did. Joe DiMaggio, Stan Musial, they never did. But they're special. It all comes down to pitching. Your pitching still has to be good. And our pitching is pretty good.

The kind of a hitter I was, I never really got into a slump. If I went 0-for-5, I'd get a couple of hits the next day, or a walk. I'd always try to get on base. But I knew how to put the ball in play. And there were a lot of us who played like that in those days. Nellie Fox, myself, and guys like that. That was our job, to occupy bases, get on. And Dominic [DiMaggio] and I did that. Of our era, you can talk to guys we played with and they'll tell you we were a pain in the neck because we just bothered them, the opponents. A lot of times you hit a ball good and it's right at somebody. But you can't stick your head in the sand and say this is going to get better because you've got to bear down a little harder. We were very lucky with the guys we had around us, Ted Williams, Bobby Doerr, a couple guys you hardly heard much of. A guy named Tom McBride [an outfielder/first baseman with the Red Sox and Senators]. He could hit left-handers like he just got out of bed.

May and June are usually when you hit a slump, and you try to make a slight change. Hopefully everything will work out and we start winning a few games here and stay eight to 10 games above. We're in a little bit of a valley now. There are going to be some changes, I think, in our approach. I think they know it, too. It's just something that happens. Of course the Yankees are playing their heads off now. We'll turn it around and it'll be tough for them because they're still seven back, and that's quite a bit. If we play .500 the rest of the way, I think we'll be safe. They have a ways to go, but I still think they've got a good ballclub. You always have to be careful of the Yankees.

Who's pitching for us tonight? [Josh] Beckett? Against the White Sox? They're the ones who were supposed to be the big ones this year. I wonder if Roland Hemond will be there. He's a nice man, one of the best in baseball. He was with that old Braves outfit. If you were around in those years, you'd have liked them.

We got a good team. The thing of it is, you just can't get down.

July 23, 2007

In one of the most devastating on-field tragedies in baseball history, Mike Coolbaugh, first-base coach for the Rockies' Double-A Tulsa Drillers, was killed yesterday when he was struck in the neck by a foul ball while standing in the first-base coach's box. Ray Chapman, who died August 17, 1920, is the only major league player killed during a game, after being hit in the head by a pitch from the Yankees' Carl Mays (a pitch that Chapman appeared not to have seen). Chapman's death led to a rule requiring umpires to replace the ball when it became dirty. It also helped, in part, to spur a rule banning the spitball. While Chapman's death emphasized the need for batting helmets, they would not become standard for several decades. Coolbaugh's death reignites the conversation requiring base coaches to wear helmets. However, a helmet likely would not have prevented the death of Coolbaugh, who was hit in the neck.

THAT'S JUST A TERRIBLE THING. AWFUL. I feel so sad for his family. It's just an awful, awful tragedy. It's something that you just don't think can ever really happen. You try to be careful out there and pay attention. But you just really don't think something like that will happen. And he was just a kid. It's awful. We started wearing batting helmets right after the war. Before that, we used to have those little skullers that went inside your hat. But I've never worn a helmet coaching the bases. You just didn't really even think of it. That was a horrible thing, that that young man was killed. I never heard of anything like that. I just didn't really even think it could happen. What a tragedy. When you're coaching first base, you've got to watch. But it's hard because you're watching the field and keeping track of what's going on. So it's hard to watch everything. Things just happen so fast. I'm very sorry about that. I'm going to say a prayer for him and his family.

The Sox beat the Indians, 6–2, in Cleveland as Jon Lester makes his first start this season after being diagnosed with anaplastic large cell lymphoma in August 2006. Lester picked up the win, going six innings and allowing two runs on five hits and three walks, striking out six. The Sox are now 60–39, holding a seven-game lead in the division over the Yankees, with the Blue Jays 11 games back, the Orioles 15½ games out, and the Devil Rays 21½ games behind.

July 31, 2007

Today is Major League Baseball's trading deadline day, when clubs can make trades without seeking waivers on players. When rumors are flying, clubhouses can become filled with tension. The Red Sox complete a trade just before the 4:00 PM deadline, sending pitcher Kason Gabbard and minor league outfielders David Murphy and Engel Beltre to Texas for reliever Eric Gagne.

WELL, THE TRADE DEADLINE, it doesn't really have a big effect on the team. You just accept it. It might cause a little tension or confusion if it goes right up to the deadline hour. But you get used to it after a couple of years. At first you're kind of wondering what's going on. But then when it's a done deal, you just accept it. It's part of the game. If you've played three or four years, you get accustomed to it. It might be a little harder on some of the younger guys who aren't used to it. We used to hate trades when we played, because we had a lot of guys play 10 years on one team, and it was hard to see them go. But sometimes it's better for a guy if he goes somewhere else. He gets a better opportunity. Just because you get traded doesn't mean you're not a good player. It just means the team had other plans. So you go to your new team and try to make the best of it.

These young guys who went, Murphy and Gabbard, hopefully they'll make the best of it and show people what they can do. I thought they were both pretty good. So hopefully they can show people that. You just can't let yourself think that being traded means you're not any good. That's not the case at all. You wouldn't

Just before the July 31 trading deadline, Boston obtained Eric Gagne from the Texas Rangers. At one time the most dominant closer in baseball, Gagne struggled with the Red Sox.

be in the big leagues, or in baseball at all, if you weren't any good. So just make the most of an opportunity. How you deal with it is going to tell a lot of people about the kind of person and the kind of player you are. Is he someone who can handle some stuff? Or does he get thrown easily? I think most people might think it's normal to take a couple of days to adjust, but then you just have to get in there and do what you can. Make the best of every opportunity that comes your way.

The Sox fall to the Orioles 5–3 at Fenway despite two home runs by David Ortiz—giving him 18 for the season—who went 3-for-4 with three RBIs and two runs scored. Josh Beckett took the loss, falling to 13–5 with a 3.41 ERA, going eight innings, allowing five runs on nine hits and two walks, and striking out six.

The Sox are 64–42, and they once again possess baseball's best record, with a .604 winning percentage, and a seven-game lead over the Yankees in the AL East. The Blue Jays are 11 games back, the Orioles 13½ games behind, and the Devil Rays 24 games out.

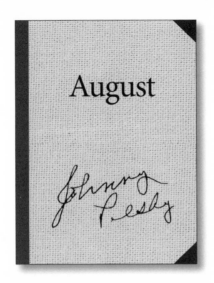

August

Johnny Pesky (signature)

August 2, 2007

The Sox take the series finale from the Orioles, 7–4, at Fenway Park as Tim Wakefield improves to 13–9 with a 4.55 ERA. Newcomer Eric Gagne makes his first appearance in a Red Sox uniform, pitching the ninth inning, allowing a run on two hits and striking out two.

The Sox are 66–42 for the season with an eight-game lead over the Yankees, followed by the Blue Jays at 12½ games out, the Orioles 15½ games back, and the Devil Rays 24½ games behind in the division.

Today is also Bobby Doerr Day at Fenway Park, with a special luncheon and a pregame ceremony honoring the Red Sox Hall of Fame second baseman. It's always a special day when one of Johnny's lifelong friends returns to Fenway. Sadly, Bobby, who turned 89 in April, thinks it will be his last trip to the historic park. The cross-country trip from his home in Oregon is getting to be too much for him.

IT WAS REALLY SPECIAL TO HAVE HIM HERE. It was a little sad, because it might be his last trip to Fenway. But he's 89. He says it's getting too hard for him to travel, and I can understand what he means by that. But then again, if they wanted him to come out, I'm sure he would. His wife is gone. She died a little bit before Ruthie did. But he's got a son out there with him, Donnie. He [Donnie] is here with his wife. But when he [Bobby] was driving around the ballpark [in a vintage convertible during the pregame ceremonies], he was really loving it. I told him, "Bobby, you got to go sign the pole." And he did. We got a picture of it.

I was very lucky. I've had some very good friends over the years from baseball. Bobby, Ted, Dom. Mickey Harris—I'm a godfather to a couple of his kids. Billy, the firstborn, called me the other day. He's a great kid. His dad was a wonderful guy, and his mom was a wonderful gal. She and Ruthie were great friends. The wives all got together when we went on the road, and they all seemed to get along pretty well.

I roomed with Vern Stephens. My first year I roomed with Bobby Doerr, and then when we made the trade with the Browns, McCarthy was the manager. He put me with Stephens. He thought I'd be an influence on him because Stephens had a reputation for being a bit of a swinger. But he was a good player. He was there every day. A tough kid, he played hard.

Two Red Sox greats, Johnny Pesky and Bobby Doerr (right), in the dugout at Fenway. The Sox paid tribute to Hall of Famer Doerr with a day in his honor on August 2, 2007.

Vern Stephens was a little taller than me. Boy, he was a handsome kid. He could knock your eyes out. He had a wonderful life and died on the golf course a few years after he stopped playing. That was a shame. He was a wonderful guy. We had a lot of fun together. You meet so many good guys in this game, you just don't forget them. I roomed with Billy Hitchcock when he was an extra here. He was a fine man. I was very lucky. Dominic was a great person, as were Bobby and outfielder Al Zarilla. Birdie Tebbetts was an outgoing guy and you couldn't help but like him. He was chirping all the time. [Tex] Hughson, [Dave] Ferris, [Joe] Dobson, Harris, Ellis Kinder, they were all great guys. Kinder drank a little bit, but he was a good guy. Hughson was a Southern gentleman. Harris was out of New York, a "dese, dose, and dem" guy. We had wonderful times.

The deal we made with the Browns, we got a lot of players but we had to give up a lot of young players. Vern Stephens, Jack Kramer. We had just gotten Babe Martin from the Browns in the minor league draft. We got Ellis Kinder in another trade. There were some good players in those deals. I thought when we got those guys, '46, '47, '48, '49, we had about as good a team as you could put on the field. But sometimes you don't always win with the best team. Sometimes there's a slip somewhere along the line. A lot of times you lose games that you should have won. That's always going to happen. I thought every team that we had in Boston was very capable of winning. We only won about three times. In '42 we did pretty well, but the war was on and we all left to go in the service. We came back in '46, we were close in '47, then '48 we were good. Those four years, '46, '47, '48, and '49, we had some great teams. We could have won three out of four of those years. It was a whole different set up then. You had to win your league to get into the World Series.

You know, it was different when we played. I think the guys that we played with were like family. Maybe it was because of the way we traveled or roomed together. I'm not sure why. But we were just so close and we really were like family. Bobby, Dom, Ted, Vern Stephens. We've stayed together all this time. I love Dominic. In fact, I owe him a phone call. We talk a couple times a week. He couldn't make it today. He's not feeling well. I sure wish he could have been here. He would have loved this. Every time I see them, it's just like old times. It's so good. And it's been wonderful over the years.

August 5, 2007

Josh Beckett improves to 14–5 with a 3.31 ERA as the Sox pick up the rubber game, 9–2, of the three-game set with the Mariners in Seattle. Beckett goes six innings, allowing a run on eight hits and two walks, while striking out nine. Manny Ramirez goes 2-for-4, including his 19th home run, with two RBIs and a run scored.

The Sox are 68–43 for a .613 winning percentage. They have a seven-game lead over the Yankees, with the Blue Jays 11½ games behind, the Orioles 15½ games out, and the Devil Rays 25½ games back.

In a bizarre scene in the fifth inning, center fielder Coco Crisp is almost run over by Seattle's mascot, Mariner Moose. As Crisp heads out to his position in the bottom of the fifth, the Moose is riding his four-wheel-drive vehicle along the warning track in front of the Red Sox's dugout. Crisp has to jump out of the way to avoid being flattened, and the vehicle clips his leg, igniting pitching coach John Farrell's rarely seen temper. The Mariners apologize for the incident after the game.

WELL, I DON'T MIND THE MASCOTS. I think they're kind of cute. And I know the kids like them. We didn't have them in our day. I don't think the great one [Ted Williams] would have liked them. You know who I'm talking about. But that guy out in Seattle was awful. He could have really hurt Coco. When you're coming out of the dugout, the last thing you're looking for is a truck going by, especially a truck driven by a moose! But I don't mind them too much. They're funny. I don't think anyone would have ever even thought about things like that in our day. I know everyone loves our guy, Wally. He's got his own fan club, and Jerry Remy makes up all those great stories about him. He hasn't run anyone over, that I know of. Let's keep it that way!

August 7, 2007

Barry Bonds hits home run Number 756, passing Hank Aaron for first place on the all-time list. Baseball fans have mixed reactions to the historic achievement.

WELL, I DIDN'T MIND HIM BREAKING THE RECORD. I knew it would be broken at some point. I just said, if he stayed healthy, he should do it. I don't know Barry Bonds, but I knew his father. His father was a fine man. He was with the Yankees. His dad was a wonderful man. It's okay that he got the record. I guess records are meant to be broken, and eventually someone will come along and break his record too. I don't know who that will be, maybe A-Rod [Alex Rodriguez]. Everyone says he's got the best chance to do it, but we'll see.

I know there's been a lot of talk about steroids, but I don't know anything about that. I just hope he didn't do anything like that. I really do. For his sake too.

Ted Williams wouldn't like it. He's not here now, so I can't speak for him, but I don't think he'd like it. No, he was a milkshake drinker. When he came to the ballpark, he was ready to play. I'm not saying he never drank. He'd have a drink once in a while later in his career. But he wasn't one of those guys who needed a drink to get him going. He was just a natural. You could always see that with Ted.

You take any good big-league player who played, nine, 12, 14, 15 years in the big leagues. When you get into that 14th or 15th year, your legs are going, you don't see the ball as well, you feel the aches and pains more. When I played—and even now—real old is, well, 38, 40, and that's young! That's young for real life! There were only a couple guys who could still do it at that age, and that's Williams and DiMaggio. A lot of guys tried it, and some of them had some success. But it's not easy at that age.

When a good player sees this coming, it's awfully discouraging. It's a little sad, because if you love the game, you want to play it forever. In a way it's cruel. But some guys adjust to it, and they can stay in the game in other ways—managing, coaching, scouting, they move into the front office. There're a lot of things you can do in this game when it's time to hang it up. I can't imagine ever doing anything else. Nope, this game has been my life, and it's been wonderful to me. I'm just going to stick it out.

The Sox lose to the Angels 10–4 in Anaheim as Tim Wakefield falls to 13–10 with a 4.81 ERA, going four innings, allowing seven runs (six earned) on seven hits, three walks, and striking out two.

The Sox are 68–45. Their once-daunting lead in the American League East is down to five games over the Yankees, with the Blue Jays 11½ games out, the Orioles 15 games back, and the Devil Rays 25½ games back.

August 13, 2007

Tim Wakefield takes a no-hitter against the Devil Rays into the seventh inning at Fenway Park before it is broken up by a Carl Crawford single to right to lead off the inning; the Sox beat Tampa Bay 3–0. With the win Wakefield is 14–10, and has earned a decision in each of his 24 starts, averaging better than six innings in each start. Wakefield is also the all-time wins leader against Tampa Bay, with 18. Jonathan Papelbon picks up his 28th save.

David Ortiz continues to demonstrate the joy and exuberance he gets from and brings to the game. Reminiscent of the playful bear hug he bestowed on Mariners second baseman Raul Ibanez on May 2 when he was caught in a double play, Ortiz demonstrates his physical fitness—as well as his sense of humor—in this game. In the sixth inning, he is knocked down by a pitch from Tampa Bay's James Shields. Face down in the dirt at home plate, rather than showing aggression, Ortiz does several push-ups (to the delight of the Fenway crowd).

The Sox are 71–47. In their last 10 games they are 5–5, while the Yankees are 9–1, creeping to within four games of the division lead. The Blue Jays are 11½ games back, with the Orioles 16½ games out and the Devil Rays 26 games back.

THE THING THAT MAKES A PITCHER like Wakefield so valuable to a team and a manager is that when you send a guy like that out there, you know you can rely on him. Getting a decision in every start isn't easy. There are so many things that can happen. A ball can fall in here and there and then the next thing you know, the hits are piling up and you're out of the game. Or you might just not feel good that day. You might just not have it that day,

Knuckleballer Tim Wakefield took a no-hitter into the seventh inning against the Devil Rays on August 13. A single that inning broke up the no-no, but the Red Sox still won 3–0.

for whatever reason. There're a lot of things at work. That's baseball. Funny things happen. But when you send a guy like that out, you know you can rely on him. You know he's going to give you a bunch of innings. It gives you a chance to rest your bullpen. So instead of having guys warming up early, you can rest them or wait until later. It makes it that much easier to plan not just for the game that day, but also the game tomorrow, because you know your bullpen is probably not going to be overworked. Some guys might even get a night off. It's very valuable to have a guy like that around.

Oh, he's great. I hope he never loses a game. He's a wonderful human being too. I think he might be second oldest to me in a Red Sox uniform now! The knuckleball is very hard to hit. I hit against a couple of them. I think we even had a left-handed knuckleballer [Mickey Haefner, with the Senators, the White Sox, and the Braves from 1943 to 1950]. I didn't do too well against the knuckleball. I doubt I could hit Wakefield in my day. If I were to try to hit him, I'd get way up in the box. Sometimes you can try to see it better and see it break. You might be able to get to the ball. You wouldn't hit it real good. That's why you don't see many guys hit home runs off a knuckleball pitcher when he's going good. Wakefield I think is one of the best knuckleball pitchers ever.

I think we had more knuckleball pitchers back then when I played. The Senators had a bunch. Washington always had good pitching. [Walt] Masterson was a good pitcher. [Ray] Scarborough. Connie Marrero. Pedro Ramos, I think it was. He was something. He won about four or five games early, and he was pitching in Washington. And, of course, he wanted to pitch to Ted. And Ted hit a home run off him. So now Pedro gets the ball and he wants Ted to sign it. So a few days later Ted hits another home run off him. Ted's rounding the bases. He says to Pedro, "Go get that sonuvabitch and I'll sign it too."

He was something, Ted was. He'd bark at you, but he loved us. Our relationship was really unusual. When we got here, the war was on and the games all were in the afternoon. We all lived over on Bay State Road [a few blocks from Fenway Park]. You walk across Kenmore Square and go to the ballpark. The four of us would sit over there in the clubhouse, and of course Ted would hold court because the year before I got here he hit .406. And oh boy, we had to listen to him. But it was very entertaining. Some of the words that would come out of his mouth, you'd think God would strike you dead. But we had so much fun. And we'd ask him a question. Sometimes when things got a little quiet and everything was nice, I'd just want to egg him on so I'd ask him a dumb question. He'd yell at me, "How stupid can you be?" Then he'd go on. Oh, you could hear him in the next block. But it was all fun.

You know what? I laughed when I saw Papi [David Ortiz] do that. He really is a one of a kind. Oh, no, I've never seen anyone like him really. Ted was a lot like him. Big, strong guy. And Ted had the big voice. But Papi is a lot different than Ted was. They're both big and strong, but Papi is a lot friendlier than Ted was. Papi is wonderful. He's just such a wonderful guy. You know what, he always hugs me. I don't think he knows how strong he is. I think he's going to break me one of these days. He hit one home run and everyone went out to greet him. I'm the last guy, and he gets down to me, and gives me a big hug. Oh, god, that was funny! He just seems to get more enjoyment out of the game than anybody I've ever seen. He truly enjoys it. He's God's gift to baseball right now because he enjoys it so much. And people love him. He could strike out or hit a home run and it would be the same with him. "Well, we'll get 'em next time." He doesn't get mad or anything like that. I love when he's going good and you hear people in the park yelling, "M-V-Papi, M-V-Papi!" Oh boy, that's a lot of fun.

I think he's more of an attraction than Ted Williams was in his day in some ways. Ted was never that friendly. This guy smiles all the time. Ted scowled all the time. You'd think, for chrissakes, he was going to go to jail. But he was okay with us. Oh, he'd yell at us, too, but that was okay. Ted, Dominic, Bobby, and me, we used to sit in the corner of the dugout where Wakefield is now, and we'd just sit and talk. It was a wonderful time.

August 14, 2007

It's an emotional day at Fenway Park as Jon Lester makes his first start at home since August 18, 2006, after being diagnosed with non-Hodgkin's lymphoma. Lester, who is not involved in the decision as the Sox stage a ninth-inning comeback to defeat the Devil Rays, 2–1, draws several standing ovations and goes seven solid innings, giving up a run on two hits and a walk and striking out four. It is his longest outing since going eight shut-out innings in a combined one-hitter (with Jonathan Papelbon) against Kansas City on July 18, 2006. He is unbeaten in his last eight major league starts.

The Sox are 72–47, holding onto baseball's best record, with a .605 winning percentage. The Yankees have fallen to five games out, with the Blue Jays 11½ games back, the Orioles 16½ games out, and the Devil Rays 27 games behind.

BOY, I'LL TELL YOU, THAT'S GREAT TO SEE. He looked really good. And even more important, he looked really healthy. This kid's got a great future in front of him. He's got really good stuff. What he went through is a tough thing. I'm sure it was tough for his parents too. But hopefully it's behind him and he can just focus on being healthy. I don't say too much to him. He's a quiet kid, a respectful kid. But when he gets out there, he's tough. He's going to be a good one. I like his stuff. He's got a lot of confidence when he's out there. He's not a cocky kid. He's confident. I just want him to be healthy.

On a sad note, word arrives at Fenway that former Yankees shortstop Phil Rizzuto died today. Johnny and Phil, both former shortstops, often drew comparisons to each other, not only for their similar builds and playing styles but also because they each remained affiliated with the team that gave them their starts in baseball. Sitting in front of his locker in the Red Sox clubhouse before the game, Johnny talks about his friend and rival.

While the two shortstops played in the oldest rivalry in baseball, it was their time together in the military that cemented their friendship and mutual respect. Each gave three years of his baseball career to serve in the navy during World War II. Rizzuto's passing makes Bobby Doerr the oldest living Hall of Fame Player.

A GOOD LITTLE PLAYER, GOOD LITTLE GUY. A friendly guy. He was my type of guy. He was a great player. I was quite surprised at how good he was until I saw him. He wasn't very big. I think he was even smaller than I was. I had a couple of inches on him, maybe a few more pounds. But he could handle a bat, could bunt, a great bunter. He could push the ball right down the line. Once in a while he hit a ball down the left-field line in Yankee Stadium.

John Lester beat the odds and delighted Boston fans when he returned to the Red Sox's starting rotation less than a year after being diagnosed with cancer.

He was as good as any shortstop that ever played. There were some guys who had better reputations, but I thought he was a better shortstop because he was a little guy, a finesse guy. Cecil Travis with Washington was a big guy. Vern Stephens with the Browns was a good shortstop.

He could run. He could run every bit as well—I think he ran better than I did. There were always comparisons about who was the best. But he won the point about who won the most. That was the Yankees. Every time we had a series with them, something would happen. It was a lot of fun. But there was no, you know, hatred, like you see with some people. We didn't have that. It was really respect. It wasn't that we hated them. It wasn't that way, because they were just nice guys. They respected us and we respected them. I don't remember ever getting into it with them. It might have been with some of the other teams. The White Sox had a couple of mean guys. Taffy Wright, I had no use for him. He was a tough guy, so I just stayed away from him. This guy was strong. You stay away from those big, strong guys. You learn a lesson.

I really got to know Phil in the navy. He went to the Naval Air Station in Virginia and we were in North Carolina for preflight. We played some games with them during the war. I really got to know him even better then. It was a good time. We were there for a while. He went on to the forward areas and I went on to get my commission. Just a nice time. It was a time when the players were pretty good guys. We had a good time with one another.

August 17, 2007

The Sox split a doubleheader with the Angels, winning the first game 8–4, then dropping the nightcap 7–5. The Sox also send outfielder Wily Mo Pena to the Nationals, ending the brief but much-maligned tenure of an outfielder whose power potential was always there, but whose ability to hit an off-speed pitch wasn't. In 2006, his first season with the Sox, the free-swinging Pena hit a highly respectable .301, going 83-for-276, with 11 home runs, but also struck out 90 times. This year he was hitting .218, 34-for-156, with 58 strikeouts and five home runs.

HE WAS ONE OF THE STRONGEST GUYS I EVER SAW. But he was just wasting away up here. He wasn't getting enough playing time and he really needs to go someplace and play. I really think he's got the ability. He just needs to develop it. He's so nice, just a sweet man. He won a couple of games for us. He hit that grand slam in Baltimore [April 26]. I think it's still going. He's one of the strongest players I've ever seen. He just needs to play. It will be interesting to see what he can do once he gets some playing time. I think he'll be okay. I hope so. I just hope he doesn't do it against us.

The Sox are 73–49, five games ahead of the Yankees, 10½ games up on the Blue Jays, 16 games ahead of the Orioles, and 26½ games up on the Devil Rays in the division.

August 18, 2007

The Sox beat the Angels, 10–5, at Fenway Park; David Ortiz's seventh career grand slam helps Curt Schilling improve to 7–5 with a 4.25 ERA.

The Sox are 74–49 with a five-game lead over the Yankees; they are 11½ games over the Blue Jays, 16 games ahead of the Orioles, and 27½ games up on the Devil Rays.

Throughout the season, the Red Sox are honoring the 1967 Impossible Dream team and recognizing milestone events from that magical season. Sadly, today marks the 40th anniversary of the saddest day of that season, and one of the saddest in the organization's history.

With two outs in the fourth inning of a scoreless game against the Angels, the right-handed hitting Tony Conigliaro,

22 in 1967, dug in. Tony C., a local legend just a few years removed from St. Mary's High in Lynn, Massachusetts—batting .287 with 20 home runs and 67 RBIs in 95 games that year—liked to crowd the plate in a time before body armor was prevalent and helmet earflaps were standard. It was the first game in which he would face Jack Hamilton, who was known to throw a spitball and liked to work inside. Hamilton's first pitch—a fastball—came in high and inside. The pitch hit Conigliaro in the face, shattering his cheekbone, and virtually ending his career.

Tony C. was rushed to Sancta Maria Hospital in Cambridge—the same hospital where another local legend and young Red Sox player Harry Agganis of Lynn, Massachusetts, had died in 1955 from a pulmonary embolism at the age of 26.

Conigliaro did not play for the rest of that Impossible Dream season, missing all of 1968 as well. He earned Comeback Player of the Year honors in 1969, but was not the same. He retired in July 1971 before attempting a short-lived comeback in 1975. He lasted just 21 games and retired for good at the age of 30.

After suffering a stroke in 1982 at the age of 37—on his way to interview for a Sox broadcasting job—Tony C. never fully recovered and died in 1990 at the age of 45.

Johnny, who was not with the Red Sox in 1967, was Tony C.'s first big-league manager, with the Sox in 1964. He and Tony's parents were also neighbors in Swampscott, Massachusetts.

HE'S PROBABLY THE BEST-LOOKING YOUNG PLAYER I ever saw. He was so good in spring training his first year, and he was on the big-league roster, and I was the manager. I'd seen him and I'd seen him work. I had a couple of good coaches. One coach I assigned to him and said, "You stay with this kid. See what happens." Every day he came back with a report, "This kid's pretty good, Johnny." Then we started playing games and I saw things. I played him in the outfield and he could run, he could throw, hitting balls all over the place. So it was cut-down time and I wanted to keep him. The general manager [Mike "Pinky" Higgins] said, "Well, he's too young." I said, "Well, look, we had a guy report here with one lung. Now we're short one out-fielder." So I was really forced to play Tony, which I would have anyway, because he looked so good. He played in the A league and hit about .340 as an 18-year-old. Now he's 19. So I'm watching this. He's running, throwing guys out. Just a great young player. I thought, "What have I got to lose?" So I played him. And I got criticized for it from some people. But I stayed with what I thought and he wound up being a pretty good player. And then he got hurt.

He lived just down the street from me. His mother and my Ruthie would play cards together. I'd come back from the ball-park, they'd be playing cards. And his dad was a wonderful guy. He went to St. Mary's in Lynn. He had a good background. There was nothing conceited about him. He was a handsome kid. He did a little singing. I thought he was going to be the next Sinatra, but it never turned out. But he was a fine player and he could do a lot of things. He only played one year in the minor leagues before he got here. He played so well, but Higgins wanted me to send him out. I said, "Mike, this kid deserves a shot." He said, "Nah, he's too young." I said, "Well, let's play him for a few weeks and see what happens." He got off to a great start and he just took right off. He didn't play much in the minor leagues because he was such a talent.

I thought he'd be a good player, but he did it so quickly. It happened so quickly. He got so good. They got rid of me, but he stayed right on and played. He was a fine player and a great kid. Very popular with the fans. Handsome, 6'3", 19 years old. The girls were running all over the place for him. His parents were wonderful folks. It was a great association.

I wasn't here when it happened, when he got hit. That happened when I was away. But I heard about it and when he was in the hospital, I went up to see him because it was kind of late in the year. His dad was very upset. We were all upset to see that kid laying in that hospital up there. It was just so sad. I thought he would have been one of the best players. Then he kind of bounced back after he got over it, but he wasn't the same. He was still a great player. If he hadn't been hit, if everything was equal, he'd be in the Hall of Fame now. That's the kind of a talent he had. He could run. He could throw. He could do everything. Even when he got hurt and came back, he worked awful hard. It looked like he was going to come back. Then, I don't know what happened to him. I used to see him when I got home, because we lived on the same block. There's no telling what he could have been, or how good he could have been, because everybody that ever saw him said "Where'd this kid come from?"

Yeah, it was sad. It was a God-given talent, but he worked at it, too. Because he knew what he wanted—he wanted to be a ballplayer so badly. He was the quickest young guy, 19 years of age, he was a star in the big leagues.

I was very fond of him. I didn't like leaving. I wanted to be here when he developed into the kind of player we thought he was going to be. And then he really got hurt and we lost him. But a fine young man. He was very devoted—not only to baseball but also to his family. His parents were great.

It was just very sad.

August 19, 2007

The Red Sox fall to the Angels 3–1 at Fenway. Julian Tavarez takes the loss despite going six solid innings, allowing two runs on two hits and two walks, and striking out two.

The Sox are 74–50, with the Yankees four games back in the East, while the Blue Jays are 10½ games out, the Orioles are 16 games back, and the Devil Rays are 26½ games out.

The Red Sox's trading-deadline acquisition, reliever Eric Gagne, has been inducing many white knuckles in Red Sox Nation. Since being acquired from the Rangers, Gagne has amassed a bloated 12.86 ERA, with a record of 1–1, two holds, and two blown saves. In today's loss to the Angels, however, Gagne shows hints of the dominating closer who did not blow a save in 2003, striking out three in the ninth inning. The ever-optimistic Johnny Pesky is confident Gagne will be able to turn around his Red Sox performance to become a key to the bullpen for the stretch run.

I THINK HE'S GOING TO BE A BIG HELP FOR US. I really do. I'm very fond of him because I saw what he was like before. And

I liked what I was seeing. I know he's had a tough time since he's come over here. But he's a good pitcher. He'll get it back on track. Hey, even Papelbon has tough outings at times, and he's the best in the business right now, in my opinion. Sometimes you just go through a tough stretch as a hitter or a pitcher. Those things happen sometimes. But you turn it around. You know the old saying, "Many are cold, but few are frozen." You turn it around eventually. When you get that ball, sometimes you have to throw the best ball as hard as you can throw. But it might be over an area of the plate where the hitter rules, and the hitter gets to it. Good pitchers will get good hitters out, they've got the advantage. Always have, always will. Except for two guys, and they were named Williams and DiMaggio. If you were a pitcher, you just hoped those guys would hit it on the ground or hit it to someone. Otherwise they were going to get you. But I really think Gagne's going to be okay. I hope so. We need him.

August 27, 2007

After completing a four-game sweep of the White Sox in Chicago, the Sox have an off day before heading to New York (with an eight-game lead over the Yankees) for a three-game showdown with the Bombers, who just lost their last two games to the Tigers.

WELL, THAT'S GOOD TO SEE. It's good to go into New York riding high. You need all the help you can get in that place. They're always tough. Especially at home. You go into that place, Yankee

Stadium, and you know what you're going to get. Those fans just love to yell and scream when the Red Sox are in. It's fun, but it's a battle. But we got Dice-K [Daisuke Matsuzaka], [Josh] Beckett, and [Curt] Schilling going. Those are our top three guys. I like our chances.

August 28, 2007

After the Sox tie the game in the top of the seventh inning, Johnny Damon unties it, giving the Yankees a 5–3 win. Matsuzaka takes the loss, dropping his record to 13–11 with a 3.88 ERA, going 6.1 innings, allowing five runs on six hits and three walks, and striking out two. Manny Ramirez leaves the game with back spasms.

The Sox are 80–52, with the Yankees seven games back in the East, the Blue Jays 13 games out, the Orioles 21 games out, and the Devil Rays 28 games back.

WELL, THAT'S A TOUGH ONE TO TAKE. But we've still got a good lead. We're still ahead, and that's where you want to be. We're in the driver's position, and the Yankees have to catch us.

August 29, 2007

The Sox fall to Roger Clemens and the Yankees, 4–3; Beckett takes the loss, going 6.2 innings, allowing four runs on 13 hits and a walk, while striking out six. Beckett falls to 16-6, with a 3.29 ERA. Clemens, meanwhile, improves to 6–5, going six innings, allowing one run on two hits and five walks, and striking out two.

The Sox are 80–53, with a six-game lead over the Yankees. The Blue Jays are 13 games back, with the Orioles 21 games out, and the Devil Rays are 27 games out.

In an odd—and ill-timed—confrontation in the second inning, with Derek Jeter on second base and Bobby Abreu at bat, an MLB official summons manager Terry Francona from the dugout to the tunnel leading to the clubhouse to ensure the manager is in compliance with baseball's uniform policy, stunning Francona.

WELL, THAT WAS STRANGE! I wasn't sure what was going on. I guess they just wanted to be sure Terry had on the right uniform. I don't think I've ever seen anything like that. But I guess they got it all straightened out. So it was no harm, no foul.

Now, if we could just get a win at Yankee Stadium! I'd feel a lot better. But I still like our chances. We've got a good lead on them. They're the ones who will have to do the work. We just have to play the way we know we can. We're going to be okay.

August 30, 2007

The Sox fall to the Yankees 5–0 at Yankee Stadium, becoming the victims of a three-game sweep in the Bronx; Chien-Ming Wang shuts down the Sox. Schilling takes the loss, dropping to 8–6 with a 4.02 ERA, going seven innings, allowing two runs on six hits and a walk, with four strikeouts. Reliever Hideki Okajima is roughed up for three runs on three hits and a walk in two-thirds of an inning.

The Sox go from sweeping four games against the White Sox in Chicago (by a combined score of 46–7) to losing three straight to the Yankees in the Bronx (by a combined score of 14–6). Their record is 80–54, and their lead over the Yankees is now down to five games. The Blue Jays are 12½ games back, the Orioles are 21 games out, and the Devil Rays are 26 games back.

How is it that a team can go from sweeping four straight to then being swept in three games in back-to-back series?

WELL, THAT HAPPENS. Sometimes I think the mystique of the New York Yankees comes out. We always compete with them. It's always a battle. But sometimes you go into that place and the strangest things just happen. Back in the '40s and '50s, we'd compete everywhere we went. Then we'd go to New York and we'd wet the bed. They've just always had good teams. They had Bobby Brown, Rizzuto, Joe Gordon, Joe DiMaggio, Roger Maris, Mickey Mantle, Gene Woodling, Yogi Berra, Elston Howard. The list just goes on and on. They had great talent. They were like the Red Sox are today. Or the Yankees are today.

But that just happens. It's just one of those silly baseball things. Once you hit a ball, you don't know what's going to happen to it. Unless you're Ted Williams or DiMaggio or those great hitters. When they hit a ball, it just seemed to find a hole. But the baseball season is all about peaks and valleys. This was a tough one, but it's just a small valley. We're going to be okay.

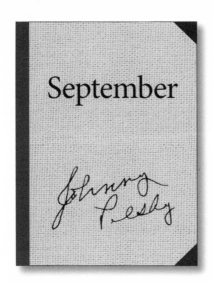

September

Johnny Pesky [signature]

September 1, 2007

In just his second major league start, Clay Buchholz delivers a stellar performance, no-hitting the Orioles at Fenway Park, the 17th no-hitter in Red Sox history and the first by a Red Sox rookie. The 23-year-old right-hander, who was called up earlier in the day as rosters expanded for the September stretch run, walks three and hits a batter in his history-making start. He struck out Baltimore's Nick Markakis on a 1–2 curveball to end the game, a 10–0 Sox win.

According to Retrosheet.org, Johnny played in two no-hitters. One was for the losing side as the Yankees' Allie Reynolds shut down the Red Sox on September 28, 1951. The next season, after Johnny had been traded to the Tigers, he was on the winning side as Virgil Trucks threw his second no-no of the season, victimizing the Yankees on August 25, 1952. Pesky was a deciding factor in Trucks' no-hitter.

I'VE REALLY ENJOYED WATCHING THE YOUNG KIDS THIS YEAR. They've been a lot of fun. Some of them really open your eyes and do things you don't expect. Now, having said that, for this kid to come up to the major leagues and throw a no-hitter in just his second start, that's just unheard of! That's amazing! I know I've never seen anything like that before.

He's from Texas. Those damn guys from Texas are all good athletes. They can throw. You look at Roger [Clemens], [Josh] Beckett, Nolan Ryan. I wonder if this kid knows what a big deal it is. There are some very good pitchers who've gone their whole careers without ever throwing a no-hitter. Curt Schilling. Roger Clemens. But I'll tell you, that was fun to watch. I'm just so happy for him. He's going to look back on that when he's my age and remember it like it was yesterday.

I played in a couple of no-hitters. I was on each side, the winners and the losers. Well, you don't like being on the team that gets no-hit, but you know, it's not easy being on the winning side either. After a few innings you figure out what's going on and you just want to play your best. You put so much pressure on yourself to do your best and not mess up.

I almost lost that no-hitter for Virgil Trucks. I would have felt awful. Early in the game [the third inning], Phil Rizzuto hit a ground ball right to me at short. It should have been an easy play, but I bobbled the ball in my glove and Rizzuto was safe at first.

A couple of innings later, the official scorer changed it to a hit. I don't know why he did. Maybe it was one of those things, upon further review. But I just felt awful. Well, then in the seventh inning, they changed it to an error again, which was the right call. The scorer even called me in the dugout during the game to find out what I thought. I told him it was an error. I bobbled it in my glove. I should have made the play. Hell, even if it was a hit, I'd have told him it was an error! A guy's got a game like that going. But it was the right call. My finger got caught in the webbing of the glove. I couldn't get a handle on the ball. All I had to do was throw the ball and I would have had him. A lot of people thought he was out, anyway. After the game, Trucks came over to thank me. I said, "For what? It was an error. I've got lots of them already. What's one more?" But I was so happy for him to get that no-hitter. He deserved it.

The Sox are 81–55, five games ahead of the Yankees in the East, with the Blue Jays 11½ games out, the Orioles 21 games back, and the Devil Rays 26 games behind.

September 3, 2007

The Sox beat the Blue Jays 13–10 at Fenway; every hitter in the Sox starting lineup has at least one hit, helping Daisuke Matsuzaka improve to 14–11 with a 4.11 ERA. Matsuzaka goes 5.1 innings, giving up seven runs on 10 hits and a walk with three strikeouts. Mike Lowell and Dustin Pedroia lead the hit parade with three each, while Lowell has four RBIs. Pedroia and Jacoby Ellsbury each score three runs.

At 83–55, the Sox are seven games up on the Yankees, 12½ games ahead of the Blue Jays, and 23 games up on the Orioles. The Devil Rays have been officially eliminated from contention.

Many local kids, including Johnny's young nephew, are heading back to school, which has Johnny reminiscing about his own school days.

MY PARENTS SENT US TO THE NUNS WHEN WE WERE KIDS. It was good. I enjoyed my school. My parents didn't have an education, so it was important to them that their kids did. I wasn't the best student, but I tried. To this day I have very good penmanship, and I have the nuns to thank for that. I like that when I sign a ball or a picture for someone, they can read my signature. Then I went to public school for high school.

When I was in the navy, we had to go to church and stuff like that. I'd get up and go to Mass, and Ted would say, "Well, I'm not going to get up. I'll give my five bucks and let 'em carry on without me." But I went all the time. I say my prayers every night, ask the good Lord for help. But that's the way I was brought up. I had nuns for teachers.

I used to play catch with my sixth-grade teacher. She was great, and she was so pretty too. I had a bit of a crush on her. I wasn't worried about her being a nun. I was just glad she could play catch. Then later, when I was playing pro ball, I'd come home and go visit her. Well, she got transferred to central Oregon. I said,

"Where's Sister Feliciano?" They told me she got transferred. It was my rookie year. I got a letter from her, and she was teaching, but she needed a phonograph or something. So I wrote back and asked her how much it cost. I don't know, maybe it was $50, $60. I didn't have a checkbook, so I got three $20 bills and I threw in another $10. I mailed it to her and she bought the thing for her class. I got the best letter. She said, "I'm saying a novena in your honor, Johnny." That's good. I can use all the help I can get.

Then another time a priest from my school made a trip to Boston, and we went to dinner. He thought it was wonderful. My first year in baseball, Rocky Mount, I didn't hear from anybody. I guess they couldn't find me. Then Louisville got a little better. Then when I got to Boston, I was quite the star. Now I'm just kidding. But I tried to maintain a dignity about not being too showy or anything, because in those years they wouldn't let you be like that. You couldn't get too high or too low. I had good people around to keep me honest.

September 8, 2007

The Sox fall to the Orioles 11–5 at Camden Yards, their only loss in the four-game series. Matsuzaka is charged with the loss, dropping his record to 14–12, as he goes a season-low 2.2 innings, giving up eight runs on six hits, including two home runs, three walks, while striking out just two. While he has shown stretches of dominance and flashes of brilliance, he is making Sox fans nervous heading into the postseason. In his last five starts, he is 1–4 with a 9.57 ERA.

The Sox are 86–57, leading the Yankees by 5½ games in the division, with the Blue Jays 13 games out. The Orioles have been officially eliminated from contention.

I THINK THE DICE COULD BE IN A LITTLE BIT OF TROUBLE. I'm a little concerned. I think with the Dice-K, it's just that he can't throw the ball as hard as he thinks he can. He's got to take a different approach, maybe throw more breaking balls. It could be the league is just getting used to him. The first two or three innings, you watch what the pitcher does. You always worry about speed, the first two times at bat, anyway. If you're a good hitter, you can hit a good fastball. But then also a good pitcher can get a good hitter out because he'll make adjustments.

A lot of guys can't hit the ball when it breaks. They didn't really have the slider before the war. It breaks probably just a few inches across the plate, whereas the curveball breaks down and away. But we never saw the slider before the war. When I got back from the navy and saw it, I thought, "Goddamn, I won't hit .100!" But I just put the bat on the ball and ran like hell!

I'm a little bit disappointed. Fourteen wins is good, but he's a better pitcher than that. He should have a few more by now, about 16. But he's had some tough luck in some games with run support. And I don't know, but he might be tired. It's a long season. Longer over here than it is in Japan. He pitches extremely well.

Our club is kind of funny. We don't have a lot of home-run hitters now. You've got Manny [Ramirez], [David] Ortiz, the third baseman, [Mike] Lowell. There're really only three guys. Most teams have four or five. It depends on how you look at a lineup. You look at the Orioles. We should beat them. You look at Tampa Bay. We should beat them, but they've got four or five pretty good players and they can beat you on a given day. And that's going to happen. You moan and groan about it but there's nothing you can do, unless you hit the ball out of the ballpark. If you hit the ball good, you think you should get a base hit. But if you hit the ball right at somebody, it's an out.

I think he'll be okay. I keep saying a baseball season is all about peaks and valleys, peaks and valleys. So maybe he's in a bit of a valley right now. But he's a good pitcher. He's a kid, but he's been doing this for a long time. He knows how to work through it. I'm sure he will. We certainly need him to.

September 10, 2007

The Devil Rays' Scott Kazmir becomes the first left-handed pitcher in 17 years to shut out the Red Sox 1–0 at Fenway Park. He is just the fourth lefty since 1957 to shut out the Sox. He also struck out 10 batters. Curt Schilling takes the loss, falling to 8–7, going six innings, giving up a run on five hits, and striking out five.

The Sox are 87–58, five games ahead of the Yankees, who have won five in a row. The Blue Jays are 14 games back.

WELL, YOU KNOW, YOU TAKE A LOOK AT TAMPA BAY, and you think we should beat them. But they've got a good team. They've got some fine young players over there. And that pitcher, he always does well against us. I don't know what it is. But he always pitches well against us. He's tough. And you run up against a pitcher like that, that's going to happen. So, when that happens, you just have to tip your hat to him and say, "Good job. We'll get you next time."

September 11, 2007

Johnny is having breakfast at the Salem Diner with the usual crew: Joe, Ray, Bob, George. They meet here every morning except Saturdays and Sundays. They sit at the end of the diner, which opened in 1941—built to look like a streamlined train car on the move—and discuss the topics of the day. They've lost a few members of the breakfast bunch over the last few years. Joe and Jack have passed on. Buzz is in a nursing home. But the group continues to meet. On this day, a gray and dreary Tuesday morning, the sixth anniversary of one of the darkest days in American history, the conversation for these friends, most of whom served in the military early in their lives, turns from politics to health to the weather and, of course, to base-ball. Johnny is at the center of the group and the center of the conversation.

IT'S GREAT COMING OVER HERE. They take wonderful care of me. Georgia, the waitress. I don't even have to place my order. She knows. We'll just sit and talk. Try to figure out the world. We take turns paying the bill. I think today might be my day.

It's a sad day today. We were all in the service at one time or another. Joe Moran, he's a war hero. It's a tough day for everyone.

There was a guy here the other day. He wanted to know what was wrong with the Red Sox. Why did they lose those three games to the Yankees? I told him not to worry about it. They're going to be fine. I think so.

I'll be heading to the game later.

The Red Sox beat the Devil Rays 16–10 at Fenway; every member of the starting lineup has multiple hits, except for catcher Kevin Cash, who delivers just one hit but three RBIs. The Sox erase a seven-run deficit in gaining the win.

The Sox are 88–58, with a five-game lead over the Yankees, who have won six in a row. The Blue Jays are 15 games out.

September 12, 2007

Kevin Youkilis has stretched his Sox record to 1,541 straight errorless chances at first base since his last miscue at the position, on July 4, 2006, at Tampa Bay. The previous mark (1,300 errorless chances) was set by Stuffy McInnis in 1921. Youkilis, who moved from third to first in 2006, has gone 183 games since his last error, an American League record. He has started 118 games at first this season, handling 1,034 chances in 128 total games without an error, also an American League record for consecutive errorless games by a first baseman in one season. That represents the most chances of any major league first baseman without an error.

Sure-handed first baseman Kevin Youkilis—until 2006 a third baseman—set team and league records for chances and games without an error during the 2007 season.

THAT'S UNUSUAL. THAT'S REALLY SOMETHING, and it's not easy to do that. He's got great hands, though, but sometimes things just happen—a bad hop, a bobble, something you just don't expect. When he was at [Single A] Lowell, they have a 10-day preseason camp. I saw him there. I saw that little [David] Eckstein too. I really liked him. I died when they let him go. He's a great little kid. Whenever he comes here, he always makes a point of saying hello and we chitchat.

I saw Youkilis there, and I thought he was good. I thought he had something then. He moved over from third to first, and that's not easy to do. But he's got good hands. You want infielders with good hands. And he works at it. He's a worker. I think sometimes people don't understand how hard it is. Sometimes you might suffer with their average, 10 or 15 points. But you get a guy who saves you a lot of runs when he's out there on the field.

Baseball is so…what's the word I'm looking for? You just can't tell what can happen. It's so unpredictable. You could throw the ball 100 miles an hour, and Christ, they're teeing off. Then you could throw a little bllllttt [raspberry sound], and they can't hit it. It's wonderful. It could drive you crazy sometimes. But if you have guys who are willing to work, you're going to be okay. Some guys have a hard time making adjustments, whether it's to pitchers or to changing positions. It's not easy, but you have to work. And Youkilis is a worker. You can't let it get to you. You just got to enjoy it.

But there are times, say if I hit two, three balls good today, well, then maybe tomorrow I'll go 0-fer. But I'll come back the next day and get a couple of hits. You don't want to go any extended period of time because then the 0-fers might start to add up. You can't let the 0-fers get you down. But that's what's great about baseball. If something bad happens, well, you can get right back out there tomorrow and try to get it straightened out. And if something good happens, well, you just try to build off it and keep it going.

I think baseball today is a lot of fun. In some ways it's even better than when we played because you got so many guys who are so good, big, and strong. The pitching is a lot different. It's just amazing. You imagine when you were playing, you thought that was it. You thought it was the best. But then you see kids today throw every bit as hard, if not harder, than pitchers did back then.

David Ortiz has two home runs, including a two-run homer in the ninth inning for his first walk-off home run of the season, giving the Sox a 5–4 victory over the Devil Rays. In his five-year Red Sox career, Ortiz has 10 walk-off home runs, including two in the 2004 postseason.

The Sox are 89–58 with a .605 winning percentage; they are five games ahead of the Yankees, who are on a seven-game winning streak. The Blue Jays are 16 games back.

DAVID ORTIZ IS ONE OF THE BEST CLUTCH HITTERS I've ever seen. It's amazing the way he just comes up with the big hits. And you know, we kind of expect that from him when he goes up there with the game on the line. We're so used to seeing him hit a huge home run and just flip his bat or get a game-winning hit. I'm actually surprised that we've gone this far into the season and this is just his first one. It seemed like last year he was doing that once a week.

Ted Williams was a great clutch hitter. He was just a great hitter, period. He was number one. But I think I'd give the benefit there to Papi [David Ortiz]. Ted got more walks than anybody, because you had to throw him a strike before he'd swing. But David has gotten some great hits for us in the last few years. And he has such a flair for the dramatic. You really know when he comes up with the game on the line or if you're behind, you've got

Johnny calls David Ortiz one of the best clutch hitters he's ever seen. In his five-year Red Sox career, "Big Papi" has hit ten walk-off home runs.

a good chance. He goes up to the plate, he walks very slowly, but he's very calm, and then all of a sudden BAM! Having guys like that on your team, well, it gives you a lot of confidence. A lot of times Ortiz just goes up there, and he seems so calm, doesn't pay attention to what's going on around him. They play that shift on him, but he can go to left field too. He's so strong, if he gets the ball off the end of his bat, it's going to hit the wall, and you got all that room over there, especially when the other team has that shift on against him. He's just so tough. And then when he does hit one of those home runs…he gave me a hug after one. Christ, I thought he was going to take my head off, he's so strong!

September 13, 2007

The Red Sox have an off day as they await the arrival of the Yankees at Fenway for a three-game series that could do much to affect the outcome of the season. The Sox hold a 5½-game lead in the East over the Yankees, who lost in Toronto last night. The Sox are 9–3 in September, including the scintillating walk-off victory two nights ago and an amazing 16–10 win (coming back from an 8–1 deficit) the night before that. The Yanks hold a slight edge in the season series over the Sox, 8–7. It is the two teams' last meeting of the regular season.

I'M REALLY LOOKING FORWARD TO THIS SERIES. It's always fun when the Yankees come to town. It's always different. There's just a different feel, a buzz. It's exciting. I'm hoping we take all three games from them. That would be fun. I always want to beat the Yankees. That could really take care of the season for us, I think. But you know what, we've got a good team. I really think this team could go all the way. I hope so, anyway.

Most citizens of Red Sox Nation hold dual citizenship in Patriot Nation. For the last several days the buzz has been about Patriot head coach Bill Belichick, recently fined by the National Football League for videotaping New York Jets coaches on the sideline at Giants Stadium in New Jersey. There are some who would say football has nothing on the ingenuity you will find in baseball when it comes to trying to get an edge.

SOME STUFF YOU'VE HEARD ABOUT FOREVER. Other stuff, who knows, maybe it was just made up. But they'd put stuff on the ball—pine tar, Vaseline, sweat, whatever—that they thought could give them an advantage. The umpires would watch. You'd hear about Ty Cobb sharpening his spikes. We didn't have that. We all had spikes anyway. We had a guy with the White Sox, Taffy Wright. Geez, I hated him! He was so mean. You'd come in and he'd kick at you. He'd try to cut you a little bit.

But we'd try stealing signs too. We didn't use a video camera. If you had said "video camera" back then, we'd have thought you dropped in from another planet. But what we'd do is, if a third-base coach could figure out what a pitcher was going to throw, he'd relay the sign to us. Billy Herman was very good at that. If it was going to be a fastball, he'd say, "Get a good pitch now." That meant a fastball was coming. "Make him throw you a good pitch" or "Make it be a strike." *Make* meant curveball. *Get* meant fastball, simple as that. With baseball players, you want to keep things simple.

But sometimes it wouldn't happen that way. Sometimes the pitcher could figure out what was going on. Once in a while you'd hear stories about someone breaking into a clubhouse or something like that. But that was more something you'd read about. And no one's going to break into a ballpark now, that's for sure. These places are locked up tighter than Fort Knox!

We'd watch the opposition. Someone would sit in the dugout and watch and see if he could figure out the signs. You're not supposed to steal the signs when you're on second base, but that was something you could try to do. But you know, some of the guys who were on second base, well, they weren't Phi Beta Kappas out there. You had to keep it simple. But a lot of times they'll give a sign and they have what they call a switch. So they give you the switch first, and then that meant it would be one of the next two or three signs. So you had to pay attention. It might be the first one, the second one, the third one. You had to study the sequence. We did things like if we thought a certain pitch was coming, we'd tap the plate with our bats one time or two times, or you put the bat back on your shoulder, little things like that. In baseball you don't want to get too smart. You've got to use your God-given ability.

September 14, 2007

Despite taking a five-run lead into the eighth inning, the Red Sox fall to the Yankees 8–7 at Fenway Park as Hideki Okajima and Jonathan Papelbon lose the lead, allowing six runs on six hits in the eighth.

The Sox, 89–59, have a 4½-game lead over the Yankees. The Blue Jays have been officially eliminated.

WELL, THAT WAS A TOUGH ONE. You think when we've got Oki and Papelbon in there, they're just going to close the door and wrap up the win for us. But this can happen. The key is to get right back out there tomorrow. They both just have to forget about it and get right back at it.

We'll be okay. I'm not worried. Don't forget, we're in the driver's seat. The Yankees are the ones chasing us.

September 15, 2007

In a showcase of potential Cy Young candidates, Josh Beckett bests Chien-Ming Wang as the Sox pound the Bombers, 10–1. Beckett improves to 19–6 with a 3.20 ERA, going seven innings, allowing a run on three hits and two walks, and striking out seven.

At 90–59, the Sox improve their lead over the Yankees to 5½ games.

THAT WAS GOOD TO SEE. WE NEEDED THAT. I'm not worried, but it's good to hold the Yankees off. One thing I've learned over the years is you can never count the Yankees out. They're always a tough team and they just keep coming back at you. You can't give them any extra help. And it's always good to beat the Yankees. Beckett pitched a great game today. I think he's going to win the Cy Young. He has to. He's been at the top of his class all year.

September 16, 2007

This will be a tough game for Johnny. Two of his favorite pitchers—Roger Clemens and Curt Schilling—are going to face off in a nationally televised game. These two titans of the mound have earned amazing credentials over the last three decades—a combined 44 years of experience, 569 wins, a .633 winning percentage, 1,275 appearances, 201 complete games, 66 shutouts,

8,156.2 innings pitched, 7,776 strikeouts, and a 3.26 ERA. They also combine for 85 years of life experience.

There are other themes to consider as well. Will this—finally—be Clemens's last appearance at Fenway Park? Will this be one of Schilling's last starts at Fenway in a Sox uniform? While Johnny is very fond of both pitchers, there is no question where his true loyalties lie and which team he wants to win.

OH, YOU KNOW, I REALLY LIKE BOTH THESE GUYS. I have such fond memories of Roger when he was here. He was just a kid when he came up. He was always so good to me. We had a lot of fun. In fact, I have a picture of the two of us at a dinner in New York a couple of years ago and he signed it "Thanks for the fun! Rocket." And he's had such a tremendous career. There really isn't anything that he hasn't done. He's got all those Cy Youngs. He was the MVP. He won a World Series. It's just a matter of time for him to go into the Hall of Fame, no question. It just depends on when he retires.

The only thing he hasn't done is throw a no-hitter. And Schilling hasn't got one, either. When you think of all the things these two guys have done and yet they haven't done that, and here comes this young kid [Clay Buchholz] who does it right out of the gate. But that's baseball; anything can happen. That's what's so great about this game.

And Schilling is so good too. You look at everything he's done, not just here but other places in his career. It's good that he's back because this is where his career started. He's a good kid. We have a lot of fun. We're always barking at each other in the clubhouse.

But it's all in good fun. I don't know what he's going to do next year. I'd love to see him come back. But you just never know. It depends on what he wants to do and what the club wants to do. But I think he's a great kid.

You know, they're both great guys, great pitchers. It's a tough game to pick sides. But really, the answer is easy. I want to see them both pitch great, but I want us to get one more run than them. Yep, that's easy.

Johnny's wish for this game doesn't come true; the Yankees score one more run than the Red Sox, winning 4–3. The Sox are 90–60, 4½ games ahead of the Yankees.

September 18, 2007

After going 2-for-4 with a run scored against the Blue Jays in Toronto, Jacoby Ellsbury's numbers for September closely resemble those of another tall, lean, left-handed phenom who once patrolled center field for the Red Sox: Fred Lynn. In 15 games as a September call-up in 1974, the 22-year-old Lynn went 18-for-43, hitting .419 with two doubles, two triples, two home runs, and 10 RBIs—a harbinger of his historic 1975 breakout season, during which he became the first player to capture both Rookie of the Year and Most Valuable Player honors. In 16 games this month, Ellsbury, who turned 24 on September 11, is hitting 22-for-55 for a .400 clip, with three doubles, a triple, three home runs, and 13 RBIs. If there is a difference in their games, it would be on the base paths. Lynn had no stolen-base attempts in his September call-up (he had 72 in his 17-year career, with a season high of 14 in 1976), while Ellsbury, who has been clocked at 3.8 seconds going down the line from home to first base, has five stolen bases this month, and six for the season.

Johnny was the first-base coach for that 1975 Red Sox team that went to the World Series, only to lose to the Cincinnati Reds in what has long been considered one of the best World Series every played.

THERE REALLY ARE A LOT OF SIMILARITIES BETWEEN THEM. They have very similar builds, both tall and thin. They're both left-handed. Both from the West Coast. Both went to Pac-10 schools. Freddie went to USC, Jacoby went to Oregon State. Both terrific players, very natural athletes. And both are very nice kids too. They're both fast. Well, I'm not sure, but I would think Ellsbury is probably faster. If it took Freddie three steps, it probably takes Jacoby two. Lynn was pretty fast, but this kid can run like the wind. I think he might be the fastest kid I've ever seen.

Lynn was such a good player, such a natural. He had so much ability. Everything was just so smooth with him. You'd see him out in center field and he just looked so graceful. He just made everything look so easy. He worked at things, but things just came so easy to him. He was a great kid. Very nice, very respectful. You had Lynn in center, [Jim] Rice in left, and [Dwight] Evans in right. That might be the best outfield we've ever had here. Every one of them was just fantastic in the field and at the plate. Rice worked so hard on his fielding. He was out there all the time, working, working. Well, now here comes Ellsbury, and he does remind me a lot of Fred Lynn.

But I'm excited for this kid. He just seems like he really knows how to play the game. He knows what needs to be done. And he looks like he's been here. He was up here earlier in the season, and I'll bet that helped him. But he just acts like he knows how to play the game the right way. I like that. I'm anxious to see how he does with a full year. I'm rooting for him.

I thought Fred Lynn and Yaz [Carl Yastrzemski] were the best left-handed hitters we had after Ted Williams. Ted, then Yaz, then Lynn. Yaz was a tremendous player. Lynn, I think, was more natural. He was a great two-way player. He could run. He could throw. A great outfielder.

Yaz was a great outfielder too. He eventually moved to first base later in his career because he could still hit. All good hitters will find a place to play. And he was a good worker. If everybody worked as hard as him, they'd be better ballplayers. I think he's great. When he goes down to our minor league camp down there in Fort Myers, if I was one of those young guys, I'd just listen to him. Just listen to everything he has to say. If he made a suggestion to you, try it. I think Yastrzemski knows as much baseball as anyone we've had.

My brother saw Jacoby play a few years ago, and told me he's going to be a terrific player. He's a nice kid. A good family. He's got that nicety about him. That's because he's from Oregon, just like Bobby Doerr, Jack Wilson. We had a lot of guys that went from the old [Pacific] Coast League who played in Portland and then went to the big leagues—Bob Johnson, who was a great guy. Ellsbury is from Madras, a little town in eastern Oregon. I played in that league when I was a kid in high school. When I saw him, I said, "Geez, where did this kid come from?" He looks so good. He's got a nice build, a nice swing. He runs so well. His arm is much better than I thought. I had to watch him for about four or five days in spring training. I can't say in one day, "This kid's going to be a star." But after watching him for a week, I knew he was special. He's got everything going for him. I liked the way he approached his at-bats. He's not trying to hit everything into the next county. His swing is nice and level. Now I can say I think he's going to be a star.

When ballplayers first come to the big leagues, I think they think they have to do a little extra. But that's not the case. Just do the things that got you here. If he just stays the same, he's going to be a star. No doubt about it. He and that little second baseman [Dustin Pedroia], they could really be good players for us.

With a 4–3 loss to the Blue Jays in Toronto, the Sox lose three in a row, cutting their division lead to 2½ games over the Yankees.

September 19, 2007

The Sox have gone 10–12, including tonight's 6–1 loss in Toronto, since Manny Ramirez left the game on August 28 in New York with a strained left oblique.

At 90–63, the Sox have lost four in a row and are 4–6 in their last 10 games. The Yankees have won four in a row and are 8–2 in their last 10. The Sox's lead, once so comfortable, is down to just 1½ games.

WE NEED MANNY [RAMIREZ] BACK IN THERE. He's such a great hitter. He's one of those guys God has been good to and given such natural talent. He can probably go a week without picking up a bat and go out and hit. He makes it look so easy, but he works at it too. He's taking batting practice right now, so hopefully he'll be back in there soon. We need him in that lineup.

He's a pretty darn good hitter. He's no Joe DiMaggio. He's no Ted Williams. And that's no knock on Manny. That's comparing the two best hitters that ever played the game. I'd say he was more like Hank Greenberg. Greenberg was a fine player. He played first base and then he went to left field, and he stuck as a left fielder. And he was strong. He was just all baseball. This guy here is a little bit of a wanderer. Sometimes you question how his thinking is.

Greenberg was a very good baseball guy. Ted Williams was a great baseball guy. You take most great players, they all understand the game of baseball. They understand the hills and valleys. Sometimes you get guys who don't understand that. And when they don't understand that, they get emotionally upset, they get almost ill. I don't mean that's Manny, but there are some guys who don't get that. Without Manny in the lineup, it just really changes things. We're a much better team with Manny in the lineup.

I think Terry has done a remarkable job in that respect, keeping the lineup strong without Manny in. Terry might do some things you might question because you're getting a secondhand look at it. I'm never going to second-guess this man because I know what he's going through. And when you're around baseball, you understand these things, because baseball is here [holds his hand up high] one day and here [holds his hand down low] the next. That's just how the game is. The key is, you've got to try to equalize it. The good teams stay at a level. They don't let themselves get too high or too low. If you make an error, someone else is there to pick you up. That's how this team is. That's the way it's always been when you have a good team.

But it hurts not having Manny in there. He's one of the game's best hitters. He's just a natural-born hitter. If he broke his leg, I think he could go out in a cast and hit. I think he's as good a right-handed hitter as we've ever had. He's proven that, hasn't he? I think he's a very fine hitter, and he's so strong, and God gave him a good body. Sometimes you get the feeling he doesn't care what's going on. You might think that. You might think he's too lackadaisical, but he's not. He loves to get that bat in his hand. He bears down. He never gives in. I love to see him up there. I know when he's up there, he's got a good chance to do something. I want to see him back up there soon. We need him. I love to see [David] Ortiz batting, and the third baseman, [Mike] Lowell, up there too. But yes, we're much better with Manny in there.

An injury to Manny Ramirez proved his value to the Red Sox: After a strained left oblique forced him out of the lineup on August 28, the team dropped 12 of their next 22 games.

September 20, 2007

This is an off day for the Sox, perhaps a welcome break after being swept by the Blue Jays in Toronto. They have now lost four in a row and are 10–8 in September. They head next to Tampa Bay for a weekend series with the Devil Rays. Their lead over the Yankees—once so comfortable at 14½ games—is down to just 1½ games. Red Sox Nation is a nervous land lately, with whispered fears of a repeat of 1978 heard everywhere. When the eternally optimistic Johnny Pesky admits to being nervous, it must be serious.

WELL, YES, I'M A LITTLE NERVOUS. I still have faith, though. I'm not worried about that. But the last few days have been tough. I've heard people talking about 1978, and I guess there's some validity to that. But that was a different team. That team was built more on offense. This team isn't like that. I think it's more well-rounded. It's got pitching, very good pitching. It's got hitters. It's got defense. I had a guy at breakfast this morning asking me what was going on. I said, "Well, what did you see on TV last night? Because that's the same thing I saw." I don't have the answers, but I know Terry and everyone else know what they're doing. I know it's going to be okay. We've got [Josh] Beckett going tomorrow for us. Their pitcher, the young lefty, [Scott] Kazmir, he's been pretty tough against us. But I think Beckett will turn it around for us.

September 21, 2007

Beckett does turn it around for the Sox—again. For the 10th time this season, he posts a win after a Red Sox loss. The Sox defeat the Devil Rays 8–1 and Beckett improves his record to 20–6 with a 3.14 ERA, 10–3 after a Sox loss. He is the major leagues' first 20-game winner of the season, and the first since 2005, when four pitchers—Florida's Dontrelle Willis (22), St. Louis's Chris Carpenter (21), the Los Angeles Angels of Anaheim's Bartolo Colon (21), and Houston's Roy Oswalt (20)—reached the milestone. Beckett is the Sox's first 20-game winner since Curt Schilling, who had 21 wins in 2004, and the 47th 20-game winner in team history. It is just the 15th time since 1950 that a Sox hurler has reached the mark.

The Sox are 91–63 with a 2½-game lead over the Yankees.

WELL, THAT WAS JUST WONDERFUL TO SEE. I know that's a special number for pitchers and really puts you up there with some very good pitchers. We had some very good pitchers in my day. I was very lucky to have them on my team. We had Tex Hughson [22–6 in 1942, 20–11 in 1946]; Dave Ferriss [21–10 in 1945, 25–6 in 1946]; Mel Parnell [25–7 in 1949]; and Ellis Kinder [23–6 in 1949]. They all won 20 games. You knew you had a pretty good chance to win a game when you had guys like that pitching for you. And you wanted to play your best to help them get a win. We had a lot of good pitching back then.

I thought we would have won more pennants than we did. We should have. We had the pitching, the hitting. But it just didn't happen. It just wasn't meant to be. But that's baseball. You can think you have the best players and the best pitchers and the best team, but that doesn't always mean anything. Sometimes, when you think back, you think the pitching was better back then. But I look at some of these guys, and they're every bit as good as the pitching was back then. I think Beckett is like that. He's a bulldog. He's hard-nosed. He's going to come at you and make you work for a hit. I like having guys like that on my team. I think Mel Parnell was probably the best pitcher I ever played with. Boy, he was good.

What was really good about Beckett's game is it stopped the losing. I knew it would stop, but you don't want it to go too long, because then you just start thinking about it too much. We needed that win last night. That was good.

September 22, 2007

The Sox come from behind with three runs in the ninth to beat the Devil Rays 8–6. Starter Daisuke Matsuzaka is not involved in the decision as much-maligned reliever Eric Gagne pitches a scoreless inning to pick up the win, giving him a record of 4–2 with a 4.01 ERA (2–2 and 7.88 with the Sox). More importantly, the Sox secure a playoff berth, the first team in either league to do so. It will be their fourth trip to the postseason in the last five years (after missing out in 2006).

The win also improves their record to 92–63, with a .594 winning percentage, reclaiming the American League's best record, which will be important in determining playoff game locations. The Sox have a 2½-game lead over the Yankees. Now the focus will be on securing their first division title since 1995—or does that matter?

THAT'S JUST WONDERFUL. I'M THRILLED. Because once you get in the playoffs, anything can happen. The important thing is to get in. I really like our chances. I think we've got a very good team. We've got great pitching, good hitting. Once we get Manny back in the lineup, we'll be even better.

I think we have a good chance if we put everything together. I think the pitching is excellent. And I think Beckett should win. If we stay close or we get a bit of a lead, we get Papelbon on the end, and he's been great. [Mike] Timlin has bounced back very, very well. He throws strikes. And of course Schilling will keep you in ballgames. He knows how to pitch. I have a lot of admiration and respect for him. When he was a kid, I don't know how he ever left here. But we got Mike Boddicker for him [as well as Brady Anderson in a trade that was finalized on July 29, 1988], and he helped us get into the playoffs. But he wasn't the answer. He wouldn't make a pimple on Schilling's butt.

I've always liked him [Schilling]. Even when he was a kid, he threw awful hard. He was gregarious, outgoing. He'll say something and get himself into trouble, but I love him. As far as I'm concerned, he's all there and I'm just crazy about him. He's a great family guy. He's a beautiful man. Beckett seems like a nice guy too. The guy that I'm really pulling for is Matt Clement, because he's got a fine arm. He could be a big help to this club if he got healthy. But I'm not sure he will in time. We'll see what happens next year.

I hope I don't sound greedy, but I would really love another ring. For some of these guys, it will be their first time in the playoffs—[Dustin] Pedroia, [Jacoby] Ellsbury, [Clay] Buchholz maybe, [Manny] Delcarmen, Coco [Crisp]. It's going to be wonderful for them.

I remember the first time we went to the playoffs. Oh, yeah, 1946. It's special. It was a wonderful feeling. We went right from playing into the World Series. We didn't have all the playoffs then. The playoffs were during the season. We won the pennant in the American League and the Cardinals won it in the National League. We won 104 games that season, and that was when it was just a 154-game season. Not bad, huh? The World Series opened in St. Louis. We won the first game. They won the second. Then we came back to Boston. We won the first game in Boston. Then they won. Then we won again in Game 5. Game 6, we went back out to St. Louis; they won that game. Then it was all tied up. Three games apiece going into the last game.

Well, we all know how it turned out. Eighth inning, the score was tied 3–3. Enos Slaughter on first. Two outs. Harry Walker hit a soft line drive to left-center. I went out to get the throw. And Slaughter was running the whole way. Never slowed down. Well, I got the throw and by the time I got the ball and threw it home, Slaughter had scored. The Cardinals won the game and they won the World Series. Everybody said I held the ball. That really bothered me because I didn't think I did. But I just let them say what they want to say. I was just so disappointed.

But I tell you, going back to St. Louis in 2004, and being down on that field and holding that trophy. Oh boy, that was something. That made up for a lot.

It's a helluva feeling to go into the playoffs. It's something you live for. You're a jock, that's why you play. A lot of guys never get into a World Series or the playoffs. So it's always special. And I'm sure if you asked any guys playing today, they'd say the same thing. Bobby [Doerr] hadn't been in one at that point. Ted [Williams] hadn't been in one. Dominic [DiMaggio] hadn't been in one. I hadn't been in one. It's not an easy thing. Our pitching staff were relatively rookies—Dave Ferriss, Joe Dobson, [Mel] Parnell came along later, Mickey Harris was a young guy.

If we don't win the division, I like the idea of the wild card. But I'd much prefer for us to win the division. That's so special. And it makes you feel good going into the playoffs. It really gives you confidence. But if we don't, I'll take the wild card. I think it's a good idea. At least it gives more teams a chance to get in now. A lot depends on which team is peaking at the right time. Just because you were the best team in July, that doesn't mean you're going to be the best team in October. Sometimes the best team doesn't always win. Look how many wild-card teams have won the World Series in the last few years. We were a wild-card team when we won in 2004. So we wouldn't have even been in without the wild card. I bet the Yankees wish there hadn't been a wild card that year! It all depends on how good your pitching is at just the right time. I like it. I think it makes things interesting. But still, I'd rather win the division. Wouldn't you? It's more special. Then you know you're in. It's a great accomplishment, but that doesn't mean you're an automatic in the playoffs.

I always say it's about peaks and valleys, and a lot depends on how you're playing going into the playoffs. Pitching will determine a lot. A lot of people say the Yankees' pitching staff is better than ours. But I don't think so. We got [Josh] Beckett, [Curt] Schilling, Dice-K [Daisuke Matsuzaka]. Our bullpen's been great. We got the young guys, [Jon] Lester and [Clay] Buchholz. No, I think we're in good shape.

The playoffs last a lot longer now. Geez, sometimes I think they'll be going till Christmas! But I just want to get them started.

September 23, 2007

Tim Wakefield (16–11, 4.73), who has the best career record of all pitchers against the Devil Rays, takes the mound. Wakefield is 19–2 lifetime against Tampa Bay and has defeated the Devil Rays six straight times since a loss on April 20, 2006. He is 4–0 in five starts against the Devil Rays this season. The last Sox pitcher to defeat one team as much as five times in one year was Luis Tiant, who went 5–1 against the Yankees in 1974. Wakefield's .905 winning percentage against Tampa Bay is second (to Houston's Roy Oswalt's .950 and 19–1 against Cincinnati) among active pitchers against one team.

I LIKE OUR CHANCES TODAY. When Wakefield gets that knuckleball really working, it's just impossible to hit. The way it moves around, it's tough to pick up. I don't know why he's been so successful against them. Sometimes, once you get a few wins against a team, your confidence just starts to build while, on the other hand, the confidence on the other team starts to go down. They start thinking, "Oh, we're facing him again. He's probably going to beat us." I'm not saying that's what's happening here, but sometimes that does happen. And he's been around so long and he's so solid. He knows what he's doing out there. Yes, I like our chances.

September 24, 2007

Tim Wakefield, who has been virtually automatic against the Devil Rays, is not able to complete the sweep at Tampa Bay and the Sox fall, 5–4, allowing the Yankees to close to 1½ games behind for the division lead. Although the Sox are in the playoffs, a division title—their first since 1995—would mean a lot.

The Sox have an off day today as they prepare for the final six games of the season, at Fenway Park against the A's and the Twins. This marks the 10th consecutive season the Sox have posted a winning record, the second-longest active streak in the majors behind the Yankees, who have a string of 15 years, including 2007. It is also the 25th season in which the Red Sox have won at least 90 games. The Sox now have six more wins this season than they achieved in all of 2006, when they finished 86–76, marking the biggest improvement from one season to the next since adding 14 victories from 78 wins in 1997 to 92 wins in 1998. The Sox have led the American League East for 159 days, going back to April 18, the longest consecutive stretch in club history. The previous record was set in 1946, when the Sox held the lead spot for the final 155 days of the season, from April 28 to Sept 29—a season that holds special memories for Johnny.

Today is also the anniversary of Johnny's last game as a player, September 24, 1954. The game was at Fenway, but Pesky was playing for the Senators, having been traded by Detroit on June 14 for Mel Hoderlein. In a concession to both his legacy in Boston and to the impending end of his playing days, Senators manager Bucky Harris inserted Johnny at shortstop as an eleventh-inning replacement for Jerry Snyder. Tom Wright had pinch hit for Snyder in the top of the inning, when the Senators scored the game's lone run. Johnny would sign as a free agent with the Orioles on December 21, 1954, but was released by the O's on April 15, 1955. It was time to move on to the next phase of his baseball life.

I GUESS I DON'T EVEN REMEMBER THAT GAME. I wasn't playing a lot by then. I do remember my first game. It was at Fenway Park, 1942. I got a couple of hits. I was happy about that. [Johnny went 2-for-4 with a triple, a sacrifice, and a run scored. The Sox beat the A's 8–3.] Well, I wasn't really sad to be done playing. I wanted to get into coaching.

Wait, you know what? I guess it was a little sad. But I was looking forward to coaching because I'd done a little bit of that when I was with Detroit. I used to come out early. I had Harvey Kuenn, Reno Bertoia, Frank Bolling. They used to call it Pesky's kiddie corps. We'd go down the left-field line. [Al] Kaline was there too. When Kaline came there, I was with him one week, and I thought, "This is the best young player I've ever seen."

Then I was Harmon Killebrew's roommate with Washington. I went in a trade from Detroit because Detroit needed a guy Washington had on their club at the Triple A level. So I went there, and they treated me good. Bucky Harris was the manager, and Mr. [Calvin] Griffith, the owner, was wonderful. It was great. And of course that winter I had done some teaching with some of the young guys. Then John McHale [former general manager and director of minor league operations for the Tigers] called me and gave me a job. And I thought for sure I'd start in Double A or something like that. I started in Class B, in Durham, North Carolina. It was my first year at Class B, and I had Dick McAuliffe, who was a great player.

I just got a note from somebody who said he was talking about his career and he mentioned my name. He said he learned a lot from me. It's always nice to hear something like that. In those years I did a lot of extra work with the young players. There were quite a few kids that I had then who eventually went to the major leagues. There were some kids who had quite a bit of experience. At that time you were only allowed so many veterans. McAuliffe was one of the best players I had. I had a center fielder. He got a lot of money to sign. He came out of Ohio State. He'd get on the bus and he'd have a stack of books. He was always reading. I said, "Why don't you read some baseball books?" And he said he was working on his degree. He was a fine player. He went from Class B to Triple A the very next year. But I think he went back to school and got his degree and then I don't know what happened to him.

I had a lot of kids there I was really fond of. A kid from Brookline, Massachusetts, name of Jim McManus, who was a first baseman. He was a swinger. He was a good player. Then I had Carl Wagner, who I thought would do better, but he went to Triple A and that was all for him.

I had good luck with young players. In fact, I did it with Jim Rice, Wade Boggs. Boggs came to me. He led the league for three or four years in a row in hitting, but they said he was a lousy fielder. He mentioned me in his Hall of Fame speech. When I heard about that, oh God, I was thrilled. That made me feel so good. I spent a lot of time with Rice too. Don Zimmer was responsible for that. He knew Rice was going to be a great player. So when Rice was with me, we worked on his running, his throwing, and his fielding. He had a good arm, but he always wanted to throw sidearm. Well, balls would tail off or take off. So we got him to come down over the top. He'd be throwing in to the second baseman and the ball would just take off. I said to him one day, "Jimmy, your arm is just so strong, when you throw the ball, it's just going to sail." So we had a routine. I'd get behind shortstop and I'd hit him ground balls, balls off the wall. Then I'd watch him throw. He'd throw sidearm and the balls would take off. And I said, "Throw the ball over the top. Even if you bounce the ball, at least he's got a chance to catch it." So he did that. We worked on it for almost two months. Every day he was out there working. An off day, he'd come out. Rice worked as hard as anyone I've ever been around. We talked about hitting. Walter Hriniak was the hitting coach, and I liked what Walter did. He was from the Charlie Lau theory of hitting. He was a very fine instructor. I was a little bit different. I had a little bit different type of swing.

All the good hitters went to Ted. He was the best hitting instructor ever. He used to watch Dominic and me, because Dominic led off and I hit second. Ted hit third. Hell, my job was just to get on base. It didn't matter how. I was walking, getting a base hit. I wound up getting 200 hits [more than 200 in each of his first three seasons]. I was on base a lot. But Ted's theory was, he was a big guy, but he didn't do all this stuff. He was straight up, he was from here to here [demonstrates a swing with the bat on a level plane]. He said if you held your hands up too high, then you had to drop down to get on the plane with the ball. That's too long a swing, and the way he explained it, he said, "Now, every ball that's thrown, it's coming at this angle." He said, "You're coming from here to here." In other words, you're taking two swings to get to one place. This way you stay right behind the ball. You take all good hitters, they stay right there, right there, right there. And you work at it and you finally convince them to do that.

Rice did that, he made that adjustment quicker than anybody I ever saw, and he became a good hitter. He was such a good hitter, he'd hit balls down the right-field line, right-center, center field. He hit balls in the center-field bleachers that were amazing. You'd think they were just going to hit the wall. But they'd take off and just keep going. And he'd hit that wall in left-center. He wasn't "pull conscious" like a lot of guys. I thought [Dwight] Evans, if he'd have done some of the things Rice did, he'd have hit more home runs. But Evans was a good player, a big, strong kid. I'd just leave him alone. When Zimmer was here, I only fooled with guys I had a pretty good shot with. Rick Miller, he was a guy like me. He'd hit the ball and he could run. Fred Lynn, he just had such ability. Sometimes you don't want to fool with guys. Other times, you see something in a guy that you think you can help.

Well, that's how I got into coaching, and I really enjoyed it. It was a little tough to retire from playing because you always think you can still play. And when you start out, you think you're going to play this game forever. And when you love the game as much as I do, you just want to keep playing. But you look in the mirror and you say, "Geez, I ache. This hurts. That hurts." But you have just enough in you that you want to stay in the game. And I loved the game and I knew I wanted to stay in it somehow. I wasn't meant for the office. I wanted to stay on the field and I liked coaching. I worked my way up. That's the only way you can do it. I started in Class B. Then I went to Single A, Double A, Triple A, and then finally when I came back to the Red Sox, I was in the big leagues. At the Triple A level, you're so close to the big leagues. You're just one step away, just like the players. A lot of clubs make changes and they might look to their Triple A club to see what they got there. The Dodgers showed an interest in me when I was working in the Pacific Coast League. I managed the Seattle club in '61 and '62. In '63 and '64 I was here. Then '65 I was with the Pirates. Then there was a change made there, and I came back here.

After I got into coaching, I never gave it a second thought as far as regrets about being done playing. But the thing I did think about is that when you have health, you can do all these things. You can go on and manage in your thirties, forties, fifties. Mr. [Connie] Mack managed in his nineties. That was amazing. He had a great life. But how many guys could do that? How many guys would want to do that? I'll be 88 this year. I don't think I want to be managing now.

September 25, 2007

As free-agent-to-be Curt Schilling perhaps winds up his Red Sox career, this playoff tune-up against the A's at Fenway Park does much to quell the nerves of an anxious nation. Schilling goes six innings, allowing just one run—a first-inning home run by September call-up Daric Barton—on six hits, while striking out six without issuing a walk, defeating the A's 7–3. Schilling nudges his record over .500, to 9–8 with a 3.87 ERA. Shannon Stewart, the first batter of the game, grounds out to short. It was the first time the two had faced each other since Stewart broke up Schilling's no-hitter with two outs in the ninth inning in Oakland in June. In a quintessential Fenway moment, in the top of the eighth inning, with Eric Gagne on the mound, a tremendous ovation spontaneously erupts in the park—a reaction to the left-field scoreboard updating the score of the Yankees' game in Tampa Bay. The Devil Rays take the lead, 6–5, in the sixth inning on a Jorge Velandia grand slam.

The win over the A's gives the Sox a 93–64 record and pushes the Yankees to three games out, with five games left to play.

BOY, WE REALLY NEEDED THAT. If we'd have lost and the Yankees won, it would be just one game and that would just be too close. I know we're in the playoffs, but I want the division. To me, that's the most important. It's just special. I'm glad we're in the play-offs but I want to say we won the division. Now we've got a little breathing room for the next few days. But we can't let our guard down. You can never do that with the Yankees because they'll just pounce on you.

September 26, 2007

The Sox beat the A's again, 11–6, sweeping the two-game series. And with a win last night over the Devil Rays, the Yankees claim a playoff spot. While the four American League playoff berths are now determined (the Sox, the Yankees, the Indians, and the Angels), no National League team has secured a playoff spot yet. The American League East title is still unclaimed, with the Sox leading the Yankees by three games. The "magic number" to clinch the division is two. A friend wants to know—good naturedly—why it seems as though the Sox enjoy torturing their fans. Can't they just win the division and let the fans take a deep breath?

The Sox and Indians have identical records, 94–64, with a .594 winning percentage.

OH SURE, THEY TORTURE THE FANS. But you know what? It's torture to the players too. They just want to get it wrapped up so they can start getting ready for the playoffs. The thing about baseball, it's not easy to play. It's not as easy as it looks, and that's good. It looks like a simple game but it's really very difficult. That's why on any given day, any team can beat another team. It doesn't always matter where you are in the standings. Things can just happen on any given day. But I know this team. The guys on this team are just as hungry to get that division title as the fans are. More so.

September 27, 2007

With the Red Sox losing to the Twins 5–4, the Yankees creep back to within two games of the American League East lead, beating the Devil Rays in Tampa Bay despite a starting lineup that includes only three of their regulars. Josh Beckett is denied the chance to post win number 21 for the season as the Sox drop the opener of their four-game, season-ending series with the Twins. The "magic number" for the Sox to clinch the AL East remains at two, with three games to play.

The Red Sox and the Indians share the American League's best record, 94–65.

Today is Johnny's 88th birthday. Perhaps it was preordained by the gods of baseball that John Michael Paveskovich would one day grow up to play for the Boston Red Sox. In a cosmic passing of the Red Sox baseball torch on September 27, 1919, Johnny was born on the day Babe Ruth played his last two games for the Red Sox, a doubleheader in Washington. Ruth angered his teammates and management by skipping the last game to play in an exhibition game in Baltimore (for which he was handsomely rewarded), as Glenn Stout and Richard Johnson wrote in the book *Red Sox Century*. In his last game with the Sox, Babe Ruth hit his 29th and final home run of the season and his first of the year in Washington, becoming the first player to hit at least one home run in every American League park during the same season.

Except for parts of three seasons spent playing with the Tigers and the Senators, and later coaching in the Yankees, Tigers, and Pirates organizations, Johnny has spent his entire career with the Red Sox. It is unlikely that the Sox—or any team—will see another player, coach, manager, broadcaster, and goodwill ambassador like Johnny Pesky.

OH, GOD, IS THAT OLD! I really haven't thought of my birthday much. Maybe it's catching up to me. I don't look forward to it. I was never that way, even when I was younger. Of course Ruthie always made a big deal out of it and we always had a party or something like that. But now I don't worry about it. I'm just always glad to have another one!

I didn't know that about Babe Ruth. On my exact birthday? No kidding. Isn't that something? That is amazing. I thought I was hatched. Well, maybe he left me in his will or something like that. That is really something, but my mother picked the Red Sox. She didn't know anything about baseball. Just liked Mr. Johnson, the Sox scout. Wow, I'd never heard that before. That is truly something. I didn't know I had that kind of a tie with the great Babe Ruth. That is pretty neat. I like having that kind of tie to him. Although I don't know what the baseball gods were thinking. You go from the greatest baseball player to me, a little Punch-and-Judy hitter. We weren't exactly in the same league.

That really is something for Red Sox history. It's interesting how it kind of came full circle like that, and here I am all these years later and I'm still with this team. And they've been just wonderful to me. Of course, Babe Ruth is the premier hitter of all time. He's still considered the greatest hitter of all time. He's better known than any other ballplayer and I think he always will be. And we've had a lot of great hitters: Hank Aaron, Ted Williams, Joe DiMaggio, Harmon Killebrew. You look back on baseball history, there're a lot of guys, but Babe was the guy who started it all. He started the home-run craze. And what a story he is. He pitched. He hit. Then he became an outfielder. He's got an amazing life history.

I never got to play with the great Babe, but I played with some great guys, and I'm quite happy with my life. Everything is nice that's happened to me, and I feel good about it. I married the right girl. We were married 60 years. When she passed, it was hard to take. But I've had a wonderful life. My boy and his wife are very good to me.

I met him [Ruth] in New York during the war. He was sick then. He was about 50, I guess. He was very nice, a very friendly fellow. It was a warm day in New York, but he had on a big coat, a nice coat. We came up from Chapel Hill to play Cleveland and the Yankees in an exhibition game for charity. Ted Williams was there, Johnny Sain, Buddy Gremp. There were a lot of guys there. Babe wasn't playing then. He was just there to watch the game. I don't think he knew much about me, because it was during the war. This must have been '43, '44, and I'd only played one year in the big leagues at that point. So I don't think he knew much about me.

Well, we came up from Chapel Hill. Dusty Cooke, who was on the Yankees as an outfielder [1930–32, then with the Red Sox 1933–36, and then with Cincinnati in 1938]. And Buddy Hassett, a first baseman who played with the Braves and the Yankees. He [Ruth] was in street clothes. He was a big guy, I guess abut 6'2". He died a few years later, '48 I think it was. He didn't give us any hitting pointers, but he had that raspy voice, and he said to me, "You're that little shortstop from Boston." I guess he studied up on us, but I was amazed he knew who I was! I couldn't believe it. That was wonderful. We played the Yankees and Cleveland. It was a bond game. They did it to raise money for war bonds, things like that.

I really thought it was a big deal to meet Babe Ruth. I'd read a lot about him as a kid. I wasn't exactly nervous; well, maybe just a little, but I was glad to meet him, thrilled. He shook my hand and I felt pretty good about that. [Mimics Ruth's raspy voice] "Hello, Kid." He had that deep voice. He was very charming. I was very impressed with him. I was impressed with his size, how big he was. I didn't think he was that big. He'd lost some weight, but he was still very tall.

And then I heard Joe Dugan, the old third baseman, talk about when he was with him on the Yankees, and what a great guy he was. Dugan said Babe took care of guys. He made all that money, so if guys were having tough times, he'd throw the money on the table and say, "Go get what you need." I'll never forget Dugan saying that. When we were kids, we didn't know much about them as players, but we got to meet them as people. Joe was a funny guy. When he stopped playing he worked for the local beer company. What a nice man he was. Dugan, after I met him, I looked him up and did some reading on him, talked to guys that played against him, like Cronin played against him, and they said he was a fine player. See, when you were from the West, like I was, you don't know about these guys, because you live out there and it's so far away. You read about them in the paper or a magazine article. But you read something, then you forget about it. There was nothing on TV, certainly no cable! No, we had crystals that we'd try to hook together and get them to work. We didn't have all the niceties that we have today.

Julio Lugo takes his 31st stolen base of the season in the eighth inning, the most by a Red Sox player since Johnny Damon's 31 steals in 2002. Since 1935, only two Sox players have stolen more than 31 bases: Tommy Harper (54 in 1973) and Otis Nixon (42 in 1994). With Coco Crisp's 27 steals this season, Lugo and Crisp have become the first two Red Sox teammates with more than 25 steals each since Tris Speaker (42) and Al Janvrin (25) back in 1914.

IF YOU CAN RUN, THAT'S SO IMPORTANT. You look at the guys on this team who can run—Coco, Lugo, Ellsbury. For years this team didn't run, and now they're a team with speed. They didn't want me to run in front of Ted. They didn't want Fred Lynn to run in front of Yaz [Carl Yastrzemski]. When I played, the only guys who could run were Dominic and me. The rest of them were all sluggers. But it's a much different game when you got guys who can run. It's fun to watch. And it can really change the game. It gives your manager options. And it makes the other manager really stop and think about who's on base for your team or who's on the bench. It's an added element.

One time I was on first base and Ted hit a ball into the triangle in center field. I didn't even have to slide when I scored. It hit in the triangle and somehow it took off down the left-field wall. I was turning third and saw the ball still rolling into the outfield. And I crossed the plate without sliding. That was fun.

September 28, 2007

Finally. After beating the Twins 5–2 at Fenway Park, the Red Sox wait in the clubhouse for the outcome of the Yankees and Orioles game at Camden Yards. As the team watches on several flat-screen TVs in the clubhouse, several thousand Red Sox fans watch the big screen in center field from their seats outside. Finally, the news arrives. Thankfully, the Orioles have come from behind to beat the Yankees 10–9 in 10 innings. Joyfully, Sox fans dance in their seats while the players dance inside under a champagne deluge. The raucous celebration moves to Fenway's infield, highlighted by Jonathan Papelbon's bizarre version of an Irish dance step. The Red Sox have captured the American League East title tonight, their first divisional crown since 1995.

The playoffs may have already been determined, but they taste sweeter secured by a divisional championship toast.

OH, THAT WAS JUST WONDERFUL TO SEE. I just can't tell you how happy I am right now. To see that kind of a celebration. That was fun. This is just wonderful. And you know what? These guys are going to remember this for the rest of their lives. I'll bet a lot of people out in the stands will remember it for the rest of their lives too. I hope so. This is just wonderful. I've been saying all year I thought this team was special. Now I know I might say that every year. But this time I really felt like this team had something. I look back to spring training, and I just can't believe how fast it went by. But I guess that's what happens when you're as old as I am. But this is just wonderful. Now we just have to get the playoffs started. We just need 11 more wins. We can do that. This team can do that. I look at the other teams in the playoffs. I think we've got just as good a chance as anybody. Why shouldn't we win? We've got good pitching, good hitting, good defense. When you get to the playoffs, it's all about pitching and defense. And we're really strong there. I think we've got a great chance. I just can't wait. Let's go.

The Sox and the Indians maintain their identical American League–best records of 95–65.

September 29, 2007

The Sox secure home-field advantage with their 6–4 win over the Twins at Fenway Park. The win gives them home-field advantage throughout the playoffs and allows them to choose the starting day of their American League Division series against the Angels.

THIS IS JUST WONDERFUL. With fans like the Red Sox Nation and a park like Fenway, you just have no idea how important home-field advantage is. I'm really looking forward to this. I really like our chances. I always say a baseball season is all about peaks and valleys, and I really feel like we're going through one of the peaks at just the right time.

September 30, 2007

The final day of the season. The Sox lose to the Twins 3–2 at Fenway.

BOY, THAT WAS FUN! I'm always amazed at how fast the baseball season goes by. It seems like I was just heading down to Florida last week. But we're still playing. That's good! We did it. We got into the playoffs. From here, anything can happen. We saw that in '04. When everything looked bad and it looked like we were done, they turned it around, swept the Yankees, and then swept the Cardinals. Anything is possible. I'd like to get another ring and then maybe I'll cut it off. Maybe I'll retire. But then again, I don't know. Maybe I'll just stick around forever.

October 2, 2007

The Red Sox return to the postseason tomorrow night for the fourth time in the last five seasons, also qualifying in 2003, 2004, and 2005, matching the Yankees as the only other major league team with four playoff appearances in that stretch. This is the 18th time in club history that the Sox will play in the postseason, third-most all-time among American League teams (behind the Yankees, with 47 post-season appearances, and the A's, with 23). This is the 10th postseason appearance for the Red Sox since 1986, when the Sox lost to the Mets in a heartbreaking World Series that still resonates in Red Sox Nation.

The Sox hold home-field advantage throughout the post-season thanks to their major-league-best record and the American League's win in the All-Star Game. Although the Sox and the Indians finished with identical 96–66 records, should both teams advance to the American League Championship Series, the Sox will still have home-field advantage by virtue of their 5–2 season-series edge over the Indians.

This will be just the second time since 1991 that the Sox will play Game 1 of a postseason series in Boston. The other time was the 2004 World Series, which they swept, 4–0, over the Cardinals.

The Sox are 62–61–1 all-time in the postseason (the lone tie coming in the 1912 World Series against the New York Giants, in which Game 2 ended in a 6–6 lock after 11 innings). The Sox are 12–11 in 23 postseason series, going 3–3 in the ALDS, 3–4 in the ALCS, and 6–4 in the World Series. The team has posted a 37–26–1 record in World Series games.

The 2004 Red Sox and the 2005 White Sox are the only teams to win eight consecutive games in a single postseason. The 2005 Red Sox are one of only two teams, along with the 2002 Diamondbacks, to be swept in the Division Series the year after winning the World Series, getting the broom in three games against the White Sox.

Since winning the American League East in 1995—their last division title—the Sox's subsequent five trips to the ALDS were as the wild-card team. The Sox's seven trips to the Division Series match the Indians, the Astros, and the Cardinals for third-most all-time (behind the Yankees, with 14, and the Braves, with 11).

While the Sox are no strangers to the postseason, it never gets old.

THIS IS THE BEST THING THAT CAN HAPPEN for a ballplayer. It really is. And if you win, it's even better. It's like going to heaven for a ballplayer. It's something that you work all year for. And for some people, it's something you work your whole life for,

In blanking the Angels 4–0 in Game 1 of the ALDS, Josh Beckett proved why he is one of baseball's most dominating pitchers once the postseason rolls around.

because it's not easy to get into the postseason. You might only get there once. So you have to make the most of it when you do. Sometimes it's harder if you get in when you're young. It's harder to understand just how hard it is if it's your first or second year because then you think it will happen every year, and that's not always the case. It's very difficult to get into the postseason. Some guys don't get in until they're almost at the end of their careers. Some guys never get in. I wish everyone could get in at least once just to see what it's like. I think maybe the older guys who get in for the first time, they might appreciate it a little bit more because they know how hard it is to get there. But that's like anything in life. You appreciate things more as you get older because you know how special it is. But this is always special. The World Series is so hard to get into. Everything has to go right for you and your team. And it's just two teams, two teams out of 30. That's not easy, that's why I just love this time of year. I'm sure glad we're here.

It's enjoyable. It's exciting. I feel good for the players. And the thing about this club is, they're really a bunch of good guys. You couldn't ask for better. You look at a guy like [Tim] Wakefield, you want him for your kid brother. [David] Ortiz, guys like that. [Josh] Beckett is a wonderful young man. [Curt] Schilling's such a good guy. The young guys, like [Dustin] Pedroia and [Jacoby] Ellsbury, they got to be just loving what's happening now. I'm very happy for all of them.

I just hope we win.

October 3, 2007   ALDS GAME 1

Josh Beckett continues his postseason dominance in Game 1 of the ALDS against the Angels at Fenway Park. Beckett is appearing in the postseason for the first time since he was named the 2003 World Series MVP, leading the Marlins to a six-game defeat of the Yankees as a 23-year-old. Beckett throws his second consecutive complete-game postseason shutout (the first came beating the Yankees in a World Series–clinching Game 6 in 2003), shutting down the Angels 4–0 on four hits, eight strikeouts, and no walks.

Boston has now taken seven straight postseason games over the Angels, going back to three in 1986 and three in 2004, and nine of its last 12 postseason games overall from the Angels.

Beckett is now the seventh pitcher in major league history to throw a complete-game shutout in back-to-back postseason starts, and the first since Orel Hershiser in Game 7 of the 1988 NLCS and Game 2 of the 1988 World Series. In seven career postseason games, six starts, Beckett is now 3–2 with a 1.74 ERA. His victory puts him into elite Red Sox company, as his complete-game shutout is the first since Luis Tiant did the same to the Reds in Game 1 of the 1975 World Series at Fenway Park.

The Sox get Angels starter John Lackey, the American League ERA leader, early, posting all their runs in the first three frames before chasing him after six innings. Kevin Youkilis's first career postseason hit, a first-inning solo home run over the Wall, turns out to be all the offense the Sox need tonight. But David Ortiz adds to the damage with a two-run homer in the third, his ninth career postseason home run, tying him with Jason Varitek for most in club history. A Mike Lowell single brings Manny Ramirez home to complete the scoring.

Ortiz's 30 postseason RBIs with the Sox are a new club record. He has now hit safely in six straight postseason games, going 8-for-22 (.364) with three doubles, two home runs, three

RBIs, four runs scored, and two walks. He has at least one hit in 19 of 21 postseason games, batting .405 (34-for-84) with six doubles, a triple, eight home runs, 26 RBIs, 18 runs scored, and four walks. His Division Series hitting streak is now at nine games.

The Sox's two-three-four hitters—Youkilis, Ortiz, and Ramirez—go a combined 5-for-10, with a double, two home runs, three RBIs, four runs scored, and two walks. Ramirez has now hit safely in 19 of his last 21 postseason games, batting .326 (28-for-86) with four doubles, five home runs, 16 RBIs, 14 runs scored, and 13 walks.

Tonight's attendance (37,597) is a Fenway Park postseason record. The crowd is also the largest ever for a Sox home play-off game since Game 5 of the 1916 World Series against the Brooklyn Robins at Braves Field.

THIS IS A VERY IMPORTANT WIN. It's very big. In a short series like this, it's very important to get the first win. It can really set the tone for the series. But I really liked our chances going into this game. Into this series, too.

That was a beautiful game Beckett pitched. He's a fine pitcher. It doesn't get much better than that. He's such a big-game pitcher. I think you take the last 20 years or so, I think you'd have to say he's one of the better pitchers who's come along. I remember when I first saw him, in spring training two years ago. I said, "Boy, where'd he come from?" I'd heard about him, but I hadn't really seen him until then, and he was very impressive. But he's been like that all year long for us. He was the best pitcher in the league. I really think so. And he's just continuing it now. He gives us such confidence when he's out there. He's a tough pitcher. He's strong, but he's mentally tough too. And those kinds of pitchers are tough to beat.

We didn't score a lot of runs tonight, but we didn't have to. Everybody came through right when we needed them. Youkilis got the home run in the first inning, and with Beckett on the mound, that was all we needed. But Papi [David Ortiz] came through like he always does. And then Mike Lowell. He's probably been the best hitter all year, the most consistent. He's so quiet. He doesn't get a lot of hype. He just goes about his business, doing things he's supposed to do to help you win.

I think you have to say we're in the driver's seat now. The Angels are certainly a good team. They've got some very good hitters over there, some very good pitchers. But I like our chances now. It's going to be a lot of fun.

October 5, 2007   ALDS GAME 2

Game 2 of the ALDS gets under way on a balmy, 79-degree Friday night with a 12 mph breeze coming in from right field.

Daisuke Matsuzaka, who has pitched on some of the baseball world's biggest stages—including the 2000 Olympics in Athens, where he became the first Japanese pitcher to be clocked at 100 mph on a radar gun; the 2004 Olympics in Sydney; and the World Baseball Classic in 2006, where he was named the tournament's Most Valuable Player as Japan won the inaugural Classic—takes the mound for the Red Sox, his first Major League Baseball postseason appearance.

But Matsuzaka's outing is disappointing. He lasts only 4.2 innings, giving up three runs on seven hits; he issued three walks and struck out three before giving way to the bullpen. Javy Lopez, Manny Delcarmen, Hideki Okajima, and Jonathan Papelbon shut down the Angels the rest of the way, joining forces to allow no runs, no hits, walking two, and striking out four.

In the end, the night belongs to Ramirez, the enigmatic Sox slugger who waits until the game is four hours and five minutes old to send the crowd of 37,706—another Fenway record, the largest crowd since World War II, and the largest postseason crowd since Game 5 of the 1916 World Series, when the Sox beat the Brooklyn Robins—home, deliriously happy, with a three-run, ninth-inning, game-winning home run, the first of his Red Sox career. The Sox beat the Angels, 6–3, taking a 2–0 series lead.

Ramirez's home run—after Ortiz was intentionally walked for the second time in the game—gave the Sox their ninth postseason walk-off win, the first since Game 5 of the 2004 ALCS against the Yankees. It is the fifth walk-off home run in Sox postseason history, and the first for Ramirez, who joins Carlton Fisk (against the Reds in the 1975 World Series), Trot Nixon (against the A's in the 2003 ALDS), and David Ortiz, who accomplished the feat twice (against the Angels in the 2004 ALDS and the Yankees in the 2004 ALCS).

Ortiz continues his postseason magic—he has hit safely in each of his last seven postseason games—going 9-for-23 (.391) with three doubles, two home runs, three RBIs, six walks, and six runs. His ALDS hitting streak continues: In 10 games he has hit .429 (15-for-35) with three home runs and nine RBIs. He has at least one hit in 20 of his last 22 postseason games, and now has 38 postseason hits in his Red Sox career, one behind Manny for most in club history. He has been intentionally walked in the ALDS six times in his career, the most in major league history. His four free passes tonight are an ALDS single-game record, and ties a major league mark, accomplished 11 times previously (the last by Ken Caminiti on October 8, 1998).

The Sox continue their postseason dominance of the Angels, running their consecutive-games winning streak to eight, including three games each in 1986 and 2004.

WELL, IT'S LOOKING REALLY GOOD NOW, ISN'T IT? What an ending! Oh wow, that was something! There was no doubt about that one, the way it just jumped off his bat. That was great! I taught him [Manny Ramirez] how to hit like that, you know! Ha! He hits more home runs in a month than I had in my career. Oh, it would be wonderful to be able to hit home runs like that. But he just knows how to hit. That's all you can say. He just knows how to hit. When he hit that one, he just went WHAM! He hits balls as far as anybody can.

I was surprised it was the first game-winning home run he's hit, because he gets so many great hits and so many big home runs. I just figured he'd have a game-winner in there somewhere. I know he's had some in the regular season, though. Well, I guess he saved it for the right time. He's a helluva hitter. He's probably as good a right-handed hitter as ever played the game.

I think you could compare him to Joe D, because he can hit like Joe. But he's not quite as selective as Joe was. Hank Greenberg, maybe. I think Jimmy Foxx would be a good comparison. They're both so damn strong. Foxx was mentally amazing. When you look at the two, I think Foxx was stronger because he had a stronger body. But Manny looks like a movie star, for crying out loud. But that hair of his, ha! That's the only thing he does that I don't like. But he's a sweetheart of a kid. He's got probably one of the best dispositions of any player in the game. He doesn't storm around. If Williams were here, he'd be cussing about this, that, and the other thing. He'd be cussing the world out. But Manny's not like that. I think Manny and Ted would have got along great. I think Ted would charm him, and vice versa. Ted would like guys like him because they could hit. Ted would probably try to correct something in his stance or watch for something on a certain pitch, after he'd hit it 450 feet. But he was great with that kind of stuff. And Manny's such a good hitter. He doesn't need a lot of help when he's locked in like he is now. But Ted could dissect a hitter better than just about anybody I ever saw. He'd look at just about any swing and find something that could help you. There was no one better for that than Ted Williams.

Diçe-K [Daisuke Matsuzaka] had a tough time tonight. They hit him too easily. His fastball seems to be straight. You take Beckett, his ball jumps at you. Schilling, it jumps at you, and he has good control. He can go there, there, there, there. But he's still got a 90-mph fastball, Schilling. And Beckett throws 95 or better. And Papelbon is even faster than that. If he throws an off-speed pitch, he's cheating himself—you're not going to hit that fastball because it comes in there so quickly. But the bullpen helped out tonight and did their stuff. That's when you know things are going good for you.

Well, we just need one more win and we're a step closer to the World Series. The Angels are a tough team, but I really think we're in good shape right now. We're in a good spot.

October 7, 2007   ALDS GAME 3

The ALDS between the Red Sox and the Angels moves to Anaheim for Game 3, with the Sox holding a 2–0 series lead. Curt Schilling, perhaps the best big-game pitcher in this postseason, takes the mound. It is his first postseason appearance since Game 2 of the 2004 World Series when, despite his bloody sock, he held the Cardinals to one run on four hits in six innings, giving the Sox their second win on their way to a four-game sweep.

Schilling lives up to his big-game reputation today, shutting out the Angels through seven innings, holding them to six hits and a walk and striking out four as the Sox clinch their ALDS victory with a 9–1 win and a three-game sweep. Of his first 25 pitches, 20 are strikes; 76 of his 100 total pitches go for strikes. Schilling runs his postseason record to 9–2, with a 1.93 ERA, in 16 postseason starts.

David Ortiz and Manny Ramirez once again lead the Sox offense, with back-to-back solo home runs in the fourth inning, before a seven-run eighth inning ends the Angels season. The Sox celebrate with champagne, beer, cigars, and Ramirez drenching everyone he can with buckets of water, while members of Red Sox Nation celebrate in the Anaheim Stadium stands for nearly 30 minutes after the game ends, hoping, to no avail, that a player will join them.

Manny's home run gives him 22 in his postseason career, tying him with Bernie Williams for the all-time lead, although Manny has done his damage in 84 games, while Williams took 121. Ortiz now has 10 postseason homers, the most in Red Sox history. It was the ninth time Ortiz and Ramirez hit back-to-back homers since becoming teammates in 2003, and the second time they've accomplished the feat in the postseason.

This victory brings the Sox's consecutive-games postseason win streak against the Angels to nine games, including three each in 1986 and 2004, matching the Yankees' nine wins over the Rangers for the longest current postseason win streak against a single team.

Red Sox pitchers post a combined 1.33 ERA, four earned runs in 27 innings, against the Angels in this series, the lowest in Division Series play since the Yankees posted a 0.33 mark in a three-game sweep of the Rangers in 1999. The record matches the seventh-lowest ERA of all time in a Division Series and gives the Sox the fourth-best record in American League history.

The series win is the eighth sweep in ALDS history, and the second by the Sox. It is the fourth time the Sox have swept a postseason series: They went 3–0 against the A's in the 1975 ALCS, 3–0 over the Angels in the 2004 ALDS, and 4–0 against the Cardinals in the 2004 World Series.

After sweeping the Angels—just as they did in 2004 on their way to their first World Series in 86 years—the Sox now await the winner of the Yankees-Indians series for Game 1 of the ALCS at Fenway Park on October 12.

WELL, THIS IS JUST WONDERFUL. I can't tell you how excited I am. It seems that everything is coming together perfectly now.

I thought the Angels would play better because they've got a very good team. They got some good pitching, some good hitters, but they can't compare with us. And they had some injuries. The guy in right field [Vladimir Guerrero] is a helluva player.

But you look around at their team, and they just can't compare to us—third base, shortstop, second base.

Schilling really showed why he's such a good player today. He got in some jams but he was able to get out of them without giving up a run. He's still a very good pitcher. He's lost a little bit of his velocity, but he's pretty smart. He's got a good mind. He's lost some of his power, but he knows how to make those adjustments. He understands baseball. He understands hitters. He understands pitching. He's really that big-game pitcher that you need. He'd have to be terrible for me not to like him. I know we still don't know what he's going to do next year, but I think there has to be a place in baseball for him. I think he has a very good baseball mind. He's the guy I want out there in these kinds of games.

Right now, everything is going right for this team, and that's the sign of a very good team. They know how to play when it gets important, when the chips are down, and right now they've got everything going for them. The pitching, the defense, the hitting. The thing is, everyone's playing well—Pedroia, Ellsbury. You watch, that kid's going to be a star. Mike Lowell, Manny, and David are always outstanding. Beckett, Schilling. Right now you really need your pitching to step up. Pitching is so much in demand at this time of year. I don't care how good your team is. If you don't have pitching, you can't win. You've got to have at least two guys on your staff who can shut somebody out. We're lucky. We have that.

David and Manny are probably the best three-four hitters, lefty-righty, I can think of. There really isn't anyone I can think of who can compare to them, the kind of hitters they are, with that kind of power. That's not very common. If you pitch around one to get to the other, well, that's just picking your poison. And nothing seems to bother them. Nothing seems to faze them. Whatever the situation, they can handle it. But it seems like when the games get more important, they both get more locked in. I'm glad they're on our side.

I can't wait to get to the next series now.

October 12, 2007   ALCS GAME 1

After a four-day layoff following the end of the ALDS, the Red Sox show little rust in the opening match of the American League Championship Series against the Indians, played in Boston; Josh Beckett, David Ortiz, and Manny Ramirez lead the way to a 10–3 victory, with everyone in the Sox starting lineup getting at least one hit.

The expected pitchers' duel between Cy Young candidates Beckett and the Indians' C.C. Sabathia never materializes, as Sabathia is chased from the game by Red Sox bats after only 4.1 innings. Ortiz and Ramirez each reach base in all 10 of their combined plate appearances, joining to go 4-for-4 with four runs scored, three RBIs, and five walks. Ortiz has reached base 16 of 18 times this postseason, going 7-for-9 with eight walks and getting hit by a pitch once. Ramirez has reached base 11 of his last 12 times at bat, going back to Game 2 of the ALDS.

Beckett holds off the Indians for six innings, allowing two runs on four hits, striking out seven, and not allowing a walk. But he is denied his third consecutive postseason shutout when

Travis Hafner gives the Indians a first-inning lead, sending a 96 mph offering from Beckett into the right-field seats. Beckett, whose career postseason record is now 4–2 with a 1.87 ERA, retires the next 10 Indians.

Cleveland's lead doesn't last long. The Sox put a run on the board in the bottom of the first before opening up the game in the third, sending nine batters to the plate. Julio Lugo doubles, then goes to third on Dustin Pedroia's bunt. The bases are loaded for Manny after Kevin Youkilis walks and Ortiz is hit by a pitch. A walk to Ramirez brings in one run, and Mike Lowell's ground-rule double accounts for two more. Jason Varitek grounds out but scores Ramirez to complete the inning's scoring.

The Sox add three runs in the fifth inning when Bobby Kielty's bases-loaded single scores Ortiz and Ramirez; next, a Varitek double scores Kielty. Boston tacks on two more runs the next inning on another bases-loaded walk to Ramirez and a sacrifice fly by Lowell.

OH, THAT WAS GREAT. That Beckett, boy, what a pitcher. I'd say he's the best pitcher in the league. I really think so. I thought it was going to be a closer game. Cleveland's got a very good team. But when you run into great pitching like that, especially at this time of year, it's tough. He was pretty much unhittable.

I really like [Indians manager] Eric Wedge. I know him from his time with us. He's a very good kid. He's smart. He knows the game. He works hard. He had a knee injury that hurt his career. I'm very happy for him to be here, but I still want us to win.

Manny and David were just fantastic. A lot of people complained about Manny this year, that maybe he wasn't playing his best or trying his hardest. But look what he's doing now. You couldn't ask for anything better. He's such a dangerous hitter. I'm glad he's on our team.

You know what I liked most about this game? Everybody got involved. David and Manny really did their thing, but everyone got into the act, too. That's very important, because you don't want to just be relying on two guys. Say if something happens, or they cool off, you want to make sure your other guys can pick it up. And everyone was in on it tonight.

Okay, so that's one. We need three more.

October 13, 2007   ALCS GAME 2

Curt Schilling takes his impressive career postseason record (9–2 with a 1.93 ERA in 16 career postseason starts) to the mound in ALCS Game 2 in Boston, facing off against Indians' right-hander and Cy Young candidate Fausto Carmona. But this time around Schilling does not produce one of his postseason gems; his outing lasts just 4.2 innings, and he gives up five runs on nine hits with three strikeouts. The Sox fall to the Indians 13–6, tying the series at a game each. Former Fenway favorite Trot Nixon, who spent 13 seasons in the Sox organization, delivers the decisive blow, a one-run, pinch-hit single off reliever Javier Lopez, as the Indians score seven runs in the eleventh inning of a five-hour, 14-minute marathon.

Ramirez continues to do his damage to opposing pitchers, belting his 23rd postseason home run in the fifth inning. Lowell follows with a solo homer, giving the Sox a 6–5 lead.

The Sox seem to have the game won in the ninth inning, when Pedroia singles with two outs. Jacoby Ellsbury pinch runs for him and steals second. Youkilis, in an 11-pitch at-bat, sends a slicing liner to center field, with Ellsbury steaming for the plate. But Grady Sizemore's sliding catch picks the ball just before it hits the ground, ending the Sox threat.

Trading-deadline acquisition Eric Gagne—whose time with the Sox has not gone well, according to Red Sox Nation—enters in the eleventh, striking out Casey Blake to start the inning before allowing a single to Sizemore and walking Asdrubal Cabrera. Nixon then singles off Lopez, scoring Sizemore. Although that will be the only run the Indians need, the Tribe adds six more, including a three-run homer by Franklin Gutierrez, as the Sox bullpen melts.

Gagne, Lopez, and Jon Lester combine to allow seven runs on five hits and two walks with two strikeouts in the eleventh as the Indians establish a new record for postseason extra-inning runs in one frame.

Ramirez and Lowell each earn three RBIs. With this game, David Ortiz has reached base safely in 10 straight postseason appearances, equaling the mark established by the Reds' Billy Hatcher in 1990.

OH MY GOD, I COULDN'T BELIEVE THAT. When I saw that last inning, I was just amazed. But the Indians swung the bat, they found holes, they hit the ball well. Their pitching was working. We hit some balls good that were caught, but we just couldn't get that run that we needed.

So many things happen when you don't expect them, or don't happen when you do. You just never know. A lot of times the best team doesn't always win. Well, that was a tough one. You know, you're going to get those stinkers every once in a while. You just hope we've got it out of our system now.

Whenever you send that big guy [Curt Schilling] to the mound, especially this time of year, you have to think you got a good chance to win. He's been so good for so long, especially in the postseason. But this is not going to be an easy series. The Indians are a good team. They're a young team, and they're hungry. You just have to make sure the Indians don't use this game as a confidence builder. They're going back home now, so they might get some momentum going. You just have to make sure you don't let them.

Oh, sure, a lot of times you score that many runs, you get a little high. You get a lot of confidence out of it. But right now, if you bear down, you can win. You just have to concentrate on the next game. You can't worry about the last game, and you can't worry about a game in a couple of days. It's just the next game. So you have to stay focused. Just worry about today, and prepare yourself mentally. Right now it's a mental thing for our guys, and rightfully so. And we've got good players. You go around the field, we've got good players at every position. And that guy [Manny Ramirez] in left field is outstanding. He can hit just about anything. I've got a lot of faith in him. I think Terry has handled this ballclub extremely well. I have faith in him too.

October 15, 2007   ALCS GAME 3

Daisuke Matsuzaka's second postseason start—in ALCS Game 3 in Cleveland—is similar to his first. Unable to get out of the fifth, he lasts just 4.2 innings, giving up four runs on six hits and two walks while striking out six. The Sox, sunk by Jake

Westbrook's sinkerball, fall to the Indians 4–2, giving a 2–1 deficit in the best-of-seven series. A despondent Matsuzaka, who declines to speak to the media after the game, sits at his locker in the visitors' clubhouse at Jacobs Field for nearly an hour after the game.

Kenny Lofton's second-inning two-run homer off Matsuzaka gives the Indians an early lead; they add two more runs in the fifth. Westbrook shuts down the Red Sox bats, inducing three inning-ending double plays—one each for October offensive monsters Ramirez and Ortiz—among 14 ground-ball outs, giving up just two runs on two hits in 6.2 innings.

In the fourth inning, Ramirez and Ortiz team up again to account for the night's oddest play as Ortiz, on second after doubling to left field, inexplicably breaks for third on Martinez's grounder. Ortiz is struck on the leg by the grounder, erasing him from the base paths.

The Sox muster only seven hits, with Jason Varitek's seventh-inning two-run homer off Westbrook accounting for their only scoring and ending Boston's 12-inning scoreless drought. The homer, Varitek's 10th career postseason round tripper, ties him with Hall of Famer Johnny Bench and Javy Lopez for most in the postseason by a catcher.

WELL, THAT WAS DISAPPOINTING. But I think he's [Matsuzaka] a pretty good pitcher. I think maybe he doesn't throw hard enough. And he's such a nice man, you just want him to do so well. It would be a good thing for him.

The key right now is to not panic. And we've got guys on this team who know that. We're only one game down. It's just that we've lost two games in a row, so that can kind of worry you. But this is a good team. The Indians are a very good team, too. I'm not taking anything away from them. But I know what we have here. We have some very good players, some very good pitchers. The key is to just go out and do what you know how to do.

We just ran into a good pitcher tonight. He pitched very well. He had the sinkerball working. He really had that going. And we were hitting the ball, but we were hitting them on the ground and right at people. We were getting guys on, but then we were hitting into double plays and ground-outs.

I think probably next year Daisuke will be a good pitcher, when he's had some time to get used to things over here, because he's a young guy, and he's got talent. It's like a kid going to high school. When you're a freshman, you don't even know your way around, but when you're a senior, you know everything. Oh, that's a terrible comparison! You'd think I was highly educated. But you know what I mean.

And we'll worry about next year next year. We get back out there tomorrow and we just got to get right back at it.

October 16, 2007   ALCS GAME 4

The Red Sox's World Series hopes seem to be fading into the October twilight as they drop ALCS Game 4 in Cleveland—their third straight postseason loss to the Indians—7–3, giving the Tribe a 3–1 series lead. Boston's position, one loss away from elimination, is precarious indeed.

If any team can come back from a 3–1 ALCS deficit, however, it would be the Red Sox. Of the 65 teams that have trailed by that margin in the postseason, only 10 have rallied to win the series—and the 2004 Sox, down 3–0 to the Yankees, were the last to accomplish the seemingly impossible feat.

The Indians' Paul Byrd, with his old-school, arm-pumping windup, stymies the Sox, allowing just two runs and striking out four without issuing a walk.

Cleveland does their damage in their 35-minute fifth inning; Casey Blake gets things started with a home run off Tim Wakefield. Franklin Gutierrez then singles and Kelly Shoppach is hit by a pitch. Sizemore's fielder's choice puts runners at the corners with one out. The usually sure-handed Youkilis drops Cabrera's foul pop—but is not charged with an error—giving a second chance to the Indians' second baseman, who then singles back to Wakefield for what looks like a sure double play. Wakefield knocks it down but is unable to get a glove on it and Gutierrez scores. Wakefield strikes out Travis Hafner, but then allows a run-scoring single (by Victor Martinez) that ends his night. Manny Delcarmen comes in, promptly giving up a three-run home run to Jhonny Peralta. Lofton, the 40-year-old out-fielder, then singles, steals second—his record 34th postseason steal—and scores on Blake's single.

By scoring seven runs in an inning twice in one series, the Indians match the 1970 Baltimore Orioles, who did it against Minnesota. The Sox answer with three runs in the fifth when Youkilis, Ortiz, and Ramirez hit back-to-back-to-back home runs, but it isn't enough.

Kevin Youkilis was charged with his first error in 1,644 chances (going back to July 4, 2006) when he mishandled a pickoff throw from Jon Lester in the sixth inning.

THERE'RE SO MANY UPS AND DOWNS IN BASEBALL. Things can really turn so quickly. And that's what we're dealing with now.

We came into this series riding so high. But we're in a little bit of trouble now.

Right now, I'm not really thinking anything. I'm very disappointed at the way some things have gone. If we lose the next one, we're out. I never dreamed this would happen. I thought our team was so good. But this has happened to us before. The Yankees beat us three in a row, then we turned around and beat them four in a row [in 2004]. But that was a different year, and a different ballclub. And this Indians team here is a pretty darned good club.

I do think we could win three in a row. If they can win the next game, then they'll come back to Fenway, and it's 3–2. Then it's a day-to-day thing. And things like that can happen. That's the funny thing about baseball. You think you've got it beat, but anything can happen. If you put everything on paper, is this guy better than that guy? We think we have the best players, but I'm sure Cleveland thinks they have the best players, too. And when the games start, it's just a roll of the dice. If you get a seven, you're in pretty good shape. If you don't, then you're behind the eight ball. That's the beauty of baseball. You never know what can happen.

Beckett will go in the next game. I'm sure he can beat them. I hope he can. I have great faith in him. He's just been superb. In the event they win that game, they've got to come back here. I don't think that will be easy for the Indians. They won three in a row. We can win three in a row just like they did. I just hope we win the next game. But Beckett's the pitcher you really want in this game. The way he's been pitching, he's just been fantastic.

They might be a little apprehensive right now, I think. But this is too good a team to give up. I'm sure they feel like they can bounce back. And if they win the next one, it will be all the better. Then they come home, they're on their own field. It's different playing at home than it is on the road, especially in the playoffs. But they've got to win one in Cleveland. You've got your best pitcher going, and we've had some luck with their guy [C.C. Sabathia].

I stay up for every pitch. I watch every pitch. I can't get to sleep unless I know how it turns out. Baseball has never put me to sleep.

October 18, 2007   ALCS GAME 5

Once again dominating in the postseason, Beckett saves the Red Sox—for at least one more game—with another playoff gem, leading the Sox to a 7–1 win over the Indians in ALCS Game 5 in Cleveland. The victory cuts the Sox's series deficit to 3–2, and sends the series back to the friendly confines of Fenway Park.

Beckett improves his postseason record to 3–0 with a 1.17 ERA, going eight innings, giving up a run on five hits, striking out a season-high 11, and allowing one walk, before giving way to Jonathan Papelbon in the ninth. Beckett, the 2003 World Series Most Valuable Player when he led the Marlins past the Yankees, improves his career postseason record to 5–2 with a 1.78 ERA.

The Red Sox offense perks up, with every starter except center fielder Coco Crisp getting at least one hit. Youkilis's first-inning solo home run off Sabathia gives the Sox a quick lead. The Indians respond in the bottom of the frame, with Sizemore scoring on Hafner's double-play grounder for the Indians' lone run.

Ramirez drew the ire of some fans on the team's off day by asking "Who cares?" if the Sox don't win. In the third inning, with Ortiz on first, he atones for his careless words with a shot to center field that hits off the top of the wall, caroming back onto the field. Believing the drive was a home run, Ramirez admires it from the batter's box before breaking into a home-run trot. The umpires, however, rule the ball to be in play, and Ramirez ends up on first with a long single, while Ortiz scores.

Beckett and Indians outfielder Lofton ignite some brief sparks in the fifth, barking at each other when Lofton flips his bat to the ground after what the outfielder thinks is ball four. After Lofton's fly out they exchange words again and the benches briefly empty, but no fisticuffs ensue. The two exchanged similar "unpleasantries" in 2005 when Beckett was with the Marlins and Lofton was with the Phillies.

The Sox add two runs in the seventh, Pedroia scoring on Youkilis's triple, which forces Sabathia from the game. The Indians starter and Cy Young candidate has had a rough series, losing both his starts to Beckett. Ortiz's sacrifice fly off Rafael Betancourt then scores Youkilis.

In the seventh, with Rafael Perez ("Raffy Left") relieving Rafael Betancourt ("Raffy Right"), J.D. Drew scores on a passed ball and Crisp scores on a bases-loaded walk to Youkilis. Another Ortiz sacrifice fly scores Lugo.

The Sox and the Indians will now return to Fenway. Will it be for one game or two?

WELL, I REALLY THINK THE MOMENTUM swings our way now, coming back to Fenway. We'll have home-field advantage, we'll have our fans here. We've just got to score some runs. If we can get an early lead, and take the Indians out of it early, that will help.

Oh, Beckett was outstanding. Just great. I wish there were more like him. But I think—I hope—Schilling will be on his game for the next game. He still throws very well, because he can go into areas on the plate where a lot of guys can't. Now he's not the same pitcher he used to be. But that's to be expected. He's been pitching for more than 20 years, and look at all the wins he's got. He's a helluva pitcher. He's very bright, and he knows he's lost some speed. But he knows how to get in around the plate. He's always had good control. He knows how to adjust. We've got some good pitchers—Delcarmen, Papelbon, [Hideki] Okajima. And especially Beckett. He's about the best in the business right now. I had a lot of confidence in him going into the game. And he showed why. I wasn't surprised he went eight innings. I thought he'd finish the game. What did he have, 11 strikeouts? He was on.

I'd say I'd compare him to Tex Hughson. Tex threw the ball hard, and had such good control. I think Beckett has a better breaking ball than Hughson. Hughson didn't have a curveball. He threw, like, a slider. But he threw awfully hard. He threw about 95, 97, 98 [mph]. You take anybody like that, they're going to be good pitchers, because I don't care how good a hitter you are, if that ball gets in on you, it's tough to hit. I think the only guy who could hit you with any consistency would be Ted Williams.

That thing that Manny said? Well, that's easy for him to say. But if you're a fan, you don't want to hear that. But you just got to take it with a grain of salt because Manny's Manny, as they say, and he's a sweet kid. And he sure knows how to hit a baseball.

Right now, they're just thinking they have to play well. They just have to relax and play like they know how. You want to think it's just another game, but it's not just another game. If we don't win, we go home. They're going to be bearing down. Trying to get a hit. As long as they get runs. Get on base and get some runs.

October 20, 2007   ALCS GAME 6

Curt Schilling resumes his stellar postseason ways for ALCS Game 6 in Boston, going seven innings, allowing two runs on six hits and striking out five without allowing a walk as the Sox pound the Indians, 12–2, forcing a Game 7. J.D. Drew emerges as the game's star, drawing the first curtain call of his inaugural Red Sox season with a first-inning grand slam off Fausto Carmona.

Schilling improves his career postseason record to 10–2 with a 2.25 ERA in 18 starts. He has never lost a game when his team has faced elimination, going 4–0 with a 1.37 ERA in five potential elimination games, while his teams have gone 5–0.

The Indians' runs come on Martinez's solo homer in the second inning and a Peralta sacrifice fly in the seventh that scores Ryan Garko, who had tripled.

Drew had a disappointing first year with the Sox, struggling to live up to his five-year, $70 million contract. Entering the game, Drew was 0-for-6 batting with runners in scoring position in the series, 1-for-11 in the postseason. He hit .237 with runners in scoring position in the regular season. But he comes through today, giving the Sox a quick lead and some much-needed breathing room.

Drew's two-out blast, scoring Pedroia, Youkilis, and Ortiz, lands in the camera well in straightaway center field. The shot is the sixth grand slam in ALCS history. The last was by Johnny Damon for the Sox in Game 7 of the 2004 series against the Yankees. Troy O'Leary also hit one for the Sox in the division series clincher against Cleveland in 1999. Drew earns another RBI in the third with a single to score Ramirez, igniting a six-run inning in which the Sox send 11 batters to the plate. Ramirez becomes the first player in LCS history to walk twice in one inning.

Another Sox player finds redemption in this game—the beleaguered Gagne pitches a one-two-three ninth, ending the game and delighting the Fenway faithful. Ellsbury makes his first start of the postseason, spelling the struggling Coco Crisp in center field. He goes 1-for-5 with a run scored and an RBI.

OH BOY, THAT WAS WONDERFUL. That was just great. I'm just thrilled. Everything went good right from the start. We got some runs right away. Schilling pitched well. When you get off to a quick lead like that, it really makes things a lot easier for your team. Your pitcher has some runs to work with. You get a little breathing room.

And Schilling knows how to pitch in these situations. He's been around for a while, and he understands things. And he's such a big-game pitcher. He doesn't get rattled. He just goes out there and does his stuff.

It was nice to see the right fielder [J.D. Drew] get some hits. He's had a tough time here this year. That was good to see. And

Right fielder J.D. Drew turned around what had been a disappointing season with his Game 6 grand slam that jump-started the Red Sox's 12–2 victory over the Indians.

even Gagne got a nice hand at the end, and he's had a tough time here this year too.

I was glad to see Ellsbury get the start. This kid's going to be something. He's what you call a blue-chipper. He can really add a spark to your lineup.

Well, it's down to one game now. The whole season comes down to one game. Anything can happen now. You really have to like this team. I know I do.

October 21, 2007　　　　　ALCS GAME 7

The Red Sox complete an amazing, improbable comeback, defeating the Indians 11–2 in ALCS Game 7 in Boston—vaulting them to their 12th American League pennant and a World Series meeting with the Rockies. Red Sox rookie Dustin Pedroia, the smallest player on the field, comes up with the biggest game of his brief Red Sox career.

Perhaps the comeback from a 3–1 series deficit is not so improbable, considering what the 2004 Sox were able to accomplish—the most unlikely comeback in ALCS history, from three games down, to sweep the next four against the Yankees.

Matsuzaka picks the right time for his first solid postseason outing, going five innings, allowing two runs, and striking out three without giving up a walk.

The Sox open the scoring with single runs in each of the first three innings. The Indians come back with solo runs in the next two frames. In the seventh inning Jacoby Ellsbury, making his second start, reaches on an error by Casey Blake, then scores on Pedroia's towering shot to the Monster seats in left-center.

The Sox blow the game open in the eighth—ending the Indians' hopes for their first World Series appearance since 1997—with six runs. Pedroia does much of the damage with a bases-loaded, three-run double. The Sox Rookie of the Year candidate finishes the night going 3-for-5, with three runs scored and five RBIs.

The postgame celebration is the expected bedlam. Papelbon once again displays his dancing skills—first debuted during the division-clincher celebration—on the infield grass, reviving his version of an Irish step dance. Ortiz stalks to the mound with the American League championship trophy, holding it aloft for all to see—few fans leave Fenway before the celebration is complete. The clubhouse is awash in champagne spray, with nary a single dry person to be found, the Sox sporting goggles to protect their eyes from the flying bubbly.

The Sox will have their work cut out for them in the World Series. The Rockies, on an impressive 10-win streak with 21 wins in their last 22 games, outscored the Red Sox 20–5 while taking two of three in their interleague meeting in June at Fenway.

Johnny Pesky is still basking in the glow of an American League championship the next day.

THAT WAS GREAT. I just can't tell you how happy I am right now. I'm on cloud nine right now. It was wonderful. I'm so happy for these guys. I thought it was well played. Guys looked very, very good, and that's what it's all about. When you play games like that, that's what it's all about.

I'm getting a lot of calls, people wishing me well. Evelyn, my friend in Oregon. My brother Vince in Oregon. A couple of local guys. I had breakfast with my gang. Now I'm just waiting for Wednesday night, to see how it goes.

Geez, that was wonderful. It was so much fun to watch. I got really drenched too. I got more stuff spilled on me. I was soaking wet when I got home. But that's okay. It was worth it. It's pretty special. I got covered in champagne. That damn Papelbon, he almost drowned me! I've had it spilled on me before, but this time I really got it. But here I am this morning, chirping like a baby robin.

Isn't it just great?

The big blow was by the little second baseman [Pedroia]. That was great. I was so happy for him. And then he drove in three more runs. What a great game for him. The whole team had a really good game. They all played real well. Papelbon. That kid second baseman. Coco Crisp made a great catch to end the game. Youkilis had a great game. Manny. David. That third baseman [Mike Lowell] is just wonderful.

I've got a really good feeling about this. I was a little nervous going into the game. The Indians only had to win one game, and we had to come back here and win two. So it was going to be easier for them. But then we tied it up 3–3; I thought we had a good chance. But you just never know. Baseball's a funny game. Anything can happen. One crazy play can turn the whole game and then who knows what will happen.

You know, I do feel for the other team. Yes, it's a tough thing, because we've all been through it. You're worried about your own success when you're on the winning side. But it's a sad thing when you lose. And they were ahead and just needed one more win. But this is a good team. They can come back like that. But Eric Wedge is a wonderful man. I feel for him. But it's a young team, and they'll be back next year. Who knows. Maybe we'll meet up with them again next October.

We played exceptionally well. We were down and came back. I really think we played a helluva series. Going to the World Series, that's the highlight of any career. Getting to the World Series ... and if you win, it's just so much better. You know, there are so many great players who never get to the World Series. It's just not easy. This will be our second trip in three years. But look how long we went without going. Any Red Sox fan knows that.

It was great last night. I got so many hugs and well wishes. Big Papi gave me a big squeeze. Papelbon, geez, I thought he was going to break my neck! I like watching the celebration. I like that stuff. It's a little crazy. It can wear at you sometimes when you get sprayed with all the champagne, but you just go home, take a shower, and it's all worth it. The players are very emotional at this time of year, too. I thought it was very well done. The owners were there, and they were great. Everyone was just thrilled.

I didn't wear those goggles. I didn't have any of that on. I didn't even know what they were at first.

I just hope things turn out good. And I'm just so happy for our fans. They've been so good, and they deserve it. And now these guys here are really folk heroes.

I'm just so happy for the players. It's so special. And I'm just happy I get to be a part of it. You know, it's a great time, a great night, and these players are going to remember this for a long time. Even when they get to be old guys, like some of us.

October 24, 2007   WORLD SERIES GAME 1

Pitcher Josh Beckett, assisted by a healthy dose of offense from the Red Sox lineup, wastes little time silencing the rolling Rockies—winners of 10 straight games and 21 of 22 outings entering the Series—as the Sox pound Colorado 13–1 in World Series Game 1 in Boston.

The Sox hold on to their momentum from the American League Championship Series win over the Indians and Beckett, the ALCS MVP, maintains his postseason dominance. In seven innings, Beckett allows one run on six hits and one walk, striking out nine. With the win over the Rockies, he is 4–0 with a 1.20 ERA in this postseason, 6–2 with a 1.73 ERA in his postseason career. In 30 innings this postseason, Beckett has allowed four earned runs on 19 hits and two walks, with 35 strikeouts.

Beckett sets the tone for the game early, striking out the first three Rockies he faces—Willy Tavares swinging, Kaz Matsui looking, and Matt Holliday swinging—all on 97 mph heat, becoming the 24th pitcher in World Series history to open a game on three straight strikeouts. He then gets Todd Helton on a swinging strikeout to start the second inning. The four straight strikeouts are the third-most in World Series history, behind the Dodgers' Sandy Koufax in 1963 and the Cardinals' Mort Cooper in 1943, both against the Yankees and both with five straight Ks.

With the win, Beckett becomes the ninth pitcher to record four wins in one postseason. No pitcher has notched five victories, a feat Beckett could accomplish in Game 5—if such a game is necessary.

Mike Timlin and Eric Gagne each pitch an inning of relief to secure the win.

The Sox pummel the Rockies with 17 hits, posting three runs in the first, one in the second, two in the fourth, and seven in the fifth, becoming the first team in postseason history to score more than 10 runs in three consecutive games.

Dustin Pedroia leads off with a home run over the Green Monster, joining Don Buford of the 1969 Orioles as the only players to open a World Series Game 1 with a home run. Pedroia is the first rookie to accomplish the feat.

The offense is well distributed—every member of the starting lineup except Jacoby Ellsbury, who scores one run and drives in another, has at least one hit. Every starter except Mike Lowell, who goes 1-for-3 with a run scored, has at least one RBI. And every starter except Julio Lugo, who goes

3-for-4 with one RBI, scores at least one run. A sampling: Kevin Youkilis goes 2-for-5 with three runs scored and one RBI; David Ortiz goes 3-for-5 with two runs scored and two RBIs; Manny Ramirez goes 3-for-4 with three runs scored and two RBIs; Jason Varitek goes 2-for-4 with one run scored and two RBIs; and J.D. Drew goes 2-for-5 with one run scored and two RBIs.

Johnny Pesky, in uniform, carries the game ball to the mound before the game.

THAT WAS WONDERFUL. I like when they score a lot of runs, especially when they score early. It makes things a lot easier for me. I can relax and not be on the edge of my seat. Beckett pitched so well. He's really the best pitcher going right now. He's the best pitcher in the American League. And he loves it out there. It's almost like when he's pitching now, it's not even a competition. I'm glad I don't have to hit against him. And I'm glad he's on our team.

They're hitting the ball exceptionally well, and everyone's getting in on it. That's really important, having everyone in. That way, if someone starts to cool off, someone else can pick it up.

[Curt] Schilling goes next and he's always very good at this time of year.

It would be wonderful to win another World Series, but I know enough to just say, "We're one game closer now." I don't want to look at it any more than that. I know how things can go in this game. But this is wonderful. And in a way I'm kind of counting on it so I can give a ring to David [Pesky's son].

As long as we win, that's all I care about. If we win the next game, that would be good, because then we go to their place, and you never know what can happen in someone else's park. We'll go out there, and if we could win [the Series] back here, that would be wonderful. But here I am saying I don't want to get too far ahead, and that's exactly what I'm doing!

October 25, 2007   WORLD SERIES GAME 2

The Red Sox bats are quieter than they were in Game 1 but the pitching is just as impressive, with Curt Schilling continuing to showcase his postseason excellence, leading the Sox to a 2–1 win over the Rockies in World Series Game 2 in Boston.

The Red Sox, winners of five straight postseason games, have a 2–0 lead over the Rockies. Of the 50 teams that have taken a 2–0 lead in World Series history, 39 have gone on to win. Of the 34 teams that have won the first two World Series games at home, 27 have gone on to win.

The Sox score single runs in the fourth and fifth innings, all the offense they will need. Lowell, who walks and goes to third on a single from Drew, scores on a sacrifice fly by Jason Varitek. In the fifth, a double by Lowell scores Ortiz, who reached base on a walk.

Schilling goes 5.1 innings, allowing one run on four hits, two walks, and a hit batter, with four strikeouts. With the win, Schilling improves to 11–2 with a 2.23 ERA in 19 career postseason starts, including his "bloody sock win" in Game 2 of the 2004 World Series, in which he went six innings against the Cardinals, helping to bring a world championship to Boston for the first time in 86 years.

World Series MVP Mike Lowell slides into third base, manned by the Rockies' Garrett Atkins, in Game 2. Lowell batted .400 in the Series, with four RBIs and six runs scored.

The "Pap-Ajima Show"—as Schilling calls it—holds the lead, and the win, for the Sox. Hideki Okajima pitches 2.1 scoreless, hitless innings, with four strikeouts. Jonathan Papelbon pitches the final 1.1 innings, giving up just one hit and striking out two. His pickoff of Holliday at first to end the eighth is the pivotal moment of the game.

Walking from the mound to the dugout after throwing his hardest pitch of the night—a 93 mph fastball that walked Todd Helton, putting two runners on with one out in the sixth inning while the Sox hold a precarious 2–1 lead—Schilling doffs his cap to the crowd, saluting the Fenway faithful, who return the gesture with a standing ovation. It is quite possible that this is the last time Schilling, a free-agent-to-be, will be seen in a Red Sox uniform on the Fenway mound.

OH, THAT WAS WONDERFUL. Now we're just two games away. Schilling is such a big-game pitcher, he's almost like money in the bank at this time of year. I was glad to see him pitch so well. I know we could lose him next year, but I'd like to see him come back.

And then the bullpen was great, almost perfect. That might have been the best Oki [Okajima] has pitched all year. And of course Papelbon is Papelbon.

We didn't hit as much as we did in the first game. I'd like a few more runs, just to make it easier to watch. But that was really a good game on both sides. You like to see those kinds of close games at this time of year.

That third baseman, Lowell, is something. He's really a catalyst for this team. He's just so solid.

Okay, so now we go out there. I'm not going. I'll stay back here and watch on TV.

October 27, 2007   WORLD SERIES GAME 3

The mile-high air in Denver does nothing to slow down the Red Sox in World Series Game 3 as they deliver a 10–5 trouncing of the Rockies for a 3–0 Series lead.

The Sox jump out early, with six runs in the third, before the Rockies post two in the sixth and three in the seventh to pull to within a run. But the Sox offense sparks again with three runs in the eighth and a run in the ninth to secure the win.

Daisuke Matsuzaka picks up the win, improving to 2–1 with a 5.03 ERA in the postseason, going 5.1 innings, and allowing two runs on three hits and three walks, with five strikeouts. Javier Lopez, Mike Timlin, Hideki Okajima, and Manny

Delcarmen hold off the Rockies until Papelbon slams the door with 1.1 scoreless innings.

Led by rookies Ellsbury (who moves into the lead-off spot, going 4-for-5 with two runs scored and two RBIs) and Pedroia (who goes 3-for-5 with a run scored and two RBIs), the Sox lineup pounds out 15 hits. Lowell goes 2-for-5 with two runs scored and two RBIs.

In the six-run third inning, Matsuzaka chips in at the plate, delivering a two-out, two-RBI single; in that same inning, Ortiz has an RBI double, Lowell gets a two-run single, and Ellsbury ties a World Series record, joining Arizona's Matt Williams as the only two players to hit two doubles in the same inning (Williams did it in 2001).

Ellsbury and Pedroia put the Sox ahead in the eighth with back-to-back doubles.

Of course the Red Sox—and their fans—know what can happen when a team is down three games to none in the postseason. The 2004 ALCS comeback is never far from their thoughts.

But if Red Sox Nation needs a confidence boost—or something to calm their nerves—consider: In World Series history, 22 teams have taken 3–0 leads, and all have gone on to win the championship. Nineteen of those 22 teams won in four games, including the last seven 3–0 situations (the 1976 Reds, the 1989 A's, the 1990 Reds, the 1998 and 1999 Yankees, the 2004 Red Sox, and the 2005 White Sox). The three other teams all won the Series by winning Game 5.

OH BOY, THAT WAS SOMETHING! I though I was going to be able to relax, but the Rockies jumped right back in it.

Oh that Ellsbury kid, he's going to be something! What a game. And that other kid, the little second baseman [Pedroia].

The two rookies did all right for themselves at the top. You like to see that, because then you say, "These are our two young guys, and they're going to be around for a while."

I thought Matsuzaka pitched extremely well. I think that's one of the best games he's pitched. He's struggled a little bit lately, but that was a good game from him.

Wow, just one more win. Isn't that something? This is wonderful. I'm still trying not to get too ahead of myself. But it's hard not to.

October 28, 2007   WORLD SERIES GAME 4

Red Sox fans don't have to wait 86 years this time to celebrate a World Series championship, as the Sox beat the Rockies, 4–3, sweeping their way to victory in World Series Game 4 in Denver.

Twenty-three-year-old Jon Lester, just a year removed from a cancer diagnosis and in his only postseason start, picks up the Series-clinching win, going 5.2 shutout innings, allowing three hits and three walks and striking out three. Delcarmen, Timlin, and Okajima bridge the innings until lights-out closer Jonathan Papelbon enters with one out in the eighth.

Papelbon goes 1.2 hitless and scoreless innings, striking out one—Seth Smith swinging on a blazing 95 mph fastball—to end the game, giving the Red Sox their seventh World Series championship and igniting a raucous celebration (minus Pap's Irish step dance) on the Coors Field lawn

Papelbon has three saves in the Series. He is 1–0 in the postseason, with four saves. In 10.2 innings over seven appearances, Papelbon allowed five hits and four walks, striking out seven. He did not allow a run in the postseason.

Mike Lowell, the World Series MVP, goes 2-for-4 with two runs scored and one RBI in the deciding game; he hit .400 (6-for-15) in the Series with three doubles, a home run, six runs scored, and four RBIs. He had a .353 mark in the postseason, with seven doubles, two home runs, 10 runs scored, 15 RBIs, and slugging .608 with a .410 OBP.

Ellsbury continues his hot streak in the lead-off spot, going 2-for-4 with a run scored. He leads off the game with a double, moves to third on a ground-out by Pedroia, and scores on a David Ortiz (1-for-3, 1 RBI) single. The Sox add single runs in the fifth as Lowell scores on a Jason Varitek (2-for-4, 1 RBI) single and adds a solo homer in the seventh.

Brad Hawpe gets the Rockies on the board in the bottom of the seventh with a solo home run off Delcarmen. Then, in his only World Series at-bat, pinch-hitter Bobby Kielty takes the first pitch he sees and deposits it into the left-field bleachers in the eighth for what would prove to be the winning margin. Down 4–1 in the bottom of the eighth, Garret Atkins's two-run home run cuts the Sox lead to 4–3—the final score.

Sweeping the Series for the second time in four years, Red Sox manager Terry Francona has never lost a World Series game.

Johnny did not make the trip to Denver, as he did in 2004 to St. Louis, preferring instead to stay at home—the home Ruthie Pesky designed when she found the plans in a magazine many years ago—and watch the games on TV with his son David, David's wife Alison, and his friend Tim.

The next morning he is back at the diner, having breakfast with his regular crew. Friends and strangers offer him congratulations and thanks. When he returns home, his phone rings seemingly nonstop with friends calling to congratulate him.

OH, I JUST CAN'T TELL YOU HOW HAPPY I AM. For a baseball player, this is heaven. There's nothing better. This is what you work so hard for. Some guys work so hard their whole lives and they never get there. It's just so special. I don't think I have the words to describe it.

I really thought back in the spring we had a chance to win. Well, I always feel that way about this club. But the way Beckett was pitching, he was the key. And it's easy to fall in love with someone like that. But his demeanor is…boy, he's all business. And Schilling, he's lost a little on his fastball, but he just knows how to pitch. Terry did a wonderful job with this team.

Evelyn called me last night. Mickey Harris's son Billy called from Florida first thing this morning. Babe Martin called me right after the game. Because even when you haven't been with a team for a long time, you still consider yourself part of the team. I'll call Dominic [Dom DiMaggio] later. I'll let Bobby [Doerr] call me—he has more money! No, I'll probably call him.

It's just been great. People are thanking me, but I didn't do anything.

You know, after waiting so long to win, it's amazing to think we only had to wait three years since the last one. I think in 2004, it had been so long, there was just so much emotion. This year is still thrilling but I don't think there's all that emotion. And that's okay, because everyone is so happy.

I was on a couple that didn't win. In '46, that was a sad thing. Christ, that was sad. Coming back from St. Louis, I don't think anyone said more than four words. And we had a good team. We were considered the favorite of the Series and we still got beat. And that just goes to show you anything can happen.

And that Lester, I was very happy for him. When he got by the first inning, I said, "This kid's going to be all right." And to think of what he's been through. This was wonderful. His demeanor is…he's very quiet. But he's very businesslike too. I like him very much.

I wanted us to score first, because when you get out in front, it just makes things a little easier. And then the other team starts trying too hard and they give you more opportunities to get them out.

I don't get nervous. Well, maybe a little nervous, because you know damn well anything can happen in a ballgame. I've seen it happen. But I just want so much for them to do well, and it was such a nail-biter, too. They caught up when we got ahead, but we were just able to hold them off. And then Kielty comes up and hits a home run in his only at-bat. He only needed one pitch too. You'd think he'd want to milk it a little more!

Everyone did so well on this team. Mike Lowell, he was the Series MVP, and he deserved it. You go right around the field: Jason Varitek, Papi, Youkilis, Pedroia, Lugo, Lowell, Manny, Coco, J.D. Drew, Ellsbury, Timlin, Papelbon, Okajima. There's not a bad guy on this team. I'm just so happy for everyone.

This is like being a kid in a candy store. If I get another ring, I'm going to give it to David, or he can have this one if he wants it. I'll keep one and he can have one, and when I die he can have both and do what he wants with them. This one doesn't fit me.

Red Sox closer Jonathan Papelbon was dominant in the postseason, pitching in seven games, earning four saves (including three in the World Series), and not giving up a single run.

It was a warm day when I got measured and my hands were swollen, but Alison put some tape on the band to make it fit. So this works. And, of course, I wear my wedding ring.

I've been very lucky and very blessed. I've had a very good life. God's been very good to me. I was blessed with good parents. I married well. I have a wonderful son. And he's got a wonderful girl. I have a wonderful family and friends. God took Ruthie when she was sick, and I'm going with a nice girl now who I was friends with when we were kids.

The only thing is now we won't have baseball for three more months, until spring training. But that's okay. I can live with that. Winning the World Series makes the off-season easy.

And I hope to be there next year, God willing.

About the Authors

Johnny Pesky

Since signing his first professional contract in 1940 in the living room of his parents' home, Johnny Pesky has served the Red Sox in virtually every capacity—All-Star player, coach, manager, broadcaster, and goodwill ambassador—over parts of seven decades. A Boston legend, Pesky has worn the uniform longer than anyone else, and his namesake "Pesky Pole" marks the right field foul line at Fenway Park.

Maureen Mullen

Maureen Mullen is a freelance writer with a long tenure covering the Boston Red Sox and Major League Baseball. A native of Lynn, Massachusetts, her work has appeared in the *Boston Globe,* the *Boston Herald,* MLB.com, *Hall of Fame Magazine,* the *Lynn Daily Item,* and many other newspapers, publications, and Web sites.